Interpreting Objects in the Hybrid Museum

Interpreting Objects in the Hybrid Museum examines the recent trend for converged collecting institutions and uses its investigation as a catalyst for critical reflection by all stakeholders on the risks, as well as advantages, of integration for cultural engagement.

Drawing on three case studies of restructured cultural organisations in Australia and New Zealand, Robinson provides valuable insights into the conceptual and practical ways in which hybridised collecting institutions operate. Reflecting on the ultimate value of converged institutions for the communities they serve, the book uncovers the dangers of misalignment between bureaucratic decision-making and the creation of cultural meaning. Actively contesting policy assumptions about the benefits of integrating museums with other kinds of cultural institutions, the book's analysis of empirical evidence provides an important counterbalance by exposing the impacts of supposedly benign structural changes to museum organisations on fundamental processes of research, documentation and contextualisation of collections.

Interpreting Objects in the Hybrid Museum highlights the consequences of policy decisions on the distinctive interpretive role of museums. As such, the book should be of interest to a range of academic and professional audiences, including scholars and students in the fields of museum and heritage studies, library and archival science, cultural studies and politics. It should also be essential reading for cultural heritage practitioners working across the museum, heritage, library, archive and gallery sectors.

Helena Robinson is a lecturer with the Museum and Heritage Studies program at the University of Sydney, Australia.

Museums in Focus
Series Editor: Kylie Message

Committed to the articulation of big, even risky, ideas in small format publications, 'Museums in Focus' challenges authors and readers to experiment with, innovate, and press museums and the intellectual frameworks through which we view these. It offers a platform for approaches that radically rethink the relationships between cultural and intellectual dissent and crisis and debates about museums, politics and the broader public sphere.

'Museums in Focus' is motivated by the intellectual hypothesis that museums are not innately 'useful,' safe' or even 'public' places, and that recalibrating our thinking about them might benefit from adopting a more radical and oppositional form of logic and approach. Examining this problem requires a level of comfort with (or at least tolerance of) the idea of crisis, dissent, protest and radical thinking, and authors might benefit from considering how cultural and intellectual crisis, regeneration and anxiety have been dealt with in other disciplines and contexts.

Recently published titles:

Sharing Authority in the Museum
Distributed Objects, Reassembled Relationships
Michelle Horwood

Interpreting Objects in the Hybrid Museum
Convergence, Collections and Cultural Policy
Helena Robinson

www.routledge.com/Routledge-Museums-in-Focus/book-series/RMIF

Interpreting Objects in the Hybrid Museum
Convergence, Collections and Cultural Policy

Helena Robinson

LONDON AND NEW YORK

First published 2019
by Routledge
2 Park Square, Milton Park, Abingdon, Oxon OX14 4RN

and by Routledge
52 Vanderbilt Avenue, New York, NY 10017

First issued in paperback 2020

Routledge is an imprint of the Taylor & Francis Group, an informa business

© 2019 Helena Robinson

The right of Helena Robinson to be identified as author of this work has been asserted by her in accordance with sections 77 and 78 of the Copyright, Designs and Patents Act 1988.

All rights reserved. No part of this book may be reprinted or reproduced or utilised in any form or by any electronic, mechanical, or other means, now known or hereafter invented, including photocopying and recording, or in any information storage or retrieval system, without permission in writing from the publishers.

Trademark notice: Product or corporate names may be trademarks or registered trademarks, and are used only for identification and explanation without intent to infringe.

British Library Cataloguing-in-Publication Data
A catalogue record for this book is available from the British Library

Library of Congress Cataloging-in-Publication Data
A catalog record has been requested for this book

ISBN 13: 978-0-367-67020-7 (pbk)
ISBN 13: 978-1-138-31869-4 (hbk)

Typeset in Times New Roman by Apex
CoVantage, LLC

Contents

	Introduction: hybrid futures?	1
1	GLAM convergence: genealogy of a concept	10
2	Same same but different: rhetorics of knowledge in the convergence debate	24
3	Process conflict: interpreting museum collections within the convergence context	41
4	Mixed messages: organisational structure and management of convergence	70
	Conclusion: Interpretive sustainability in the hybrid institution	96

Appendix 1 – case study descriptions   115
Appendix 2 – case study comparative table   125
Bibliography   127
Index   135

Anonymous graffiti, Athens. Image and logo by James Verdon (2017).

Introduction
Hybrid futures?

> *Convergence is seen by the managerial side of things as the best model, because you can pool all of your resources, put them all in one place, make all these 'savings' by making all these people operate in one group rather than three or four groups. . . . But then there's the conceptual side of things. What does convergence actually mean to the product that you're producing?*
>
> —collections and exhibitions officer, Lonehill

It's 2040 and the standalone museum no longer exists. In the absence of a self-sufficient rationale, museums have been reconceptualised as subsidiary health and social services supporting a range of educational, training, counselling, outreach and well-being programs. Through fusion with other kinds of civic organisations and various forms of hybridised practice, museums are no longer fundamentally 'collecting institutions,' but rather multidisciplinary community centres that integrate previously siloed, but no longer independently viable, public functions. In the words of the USA's Adam Rozan (2017) – audience engagement specialist, museum studies educator and self-proclaimed visitor advocate – these new institutions will absorb and stand in for essential public services at the local level:

> Each new hybrid museum represents a community that was spared from losing a library, preschool, park, house of worship, health center, and other valuable, community-dependent organizations and facilities.
> (Rozan 2017, 17)

Appearing in a special future-forecasting edition of *Museum* magazine, a publication of the American Alliance of Museums, Rozan's prediction for museums of 2040 characterises arguments presented by other contributors, decentring the role of objects in the purpose and function of museums. In this future, curators and collection managers share space with, or may be replaced by, psychologists, school teachers, artists, musicians, chaplains, librarians, engineers, start-up entrepreneurs and social workers. The collection-focussed scholar-curator is perceived as a largely self-serving, increasingly isolated figure fast approaching obsolescence.

Arguably, this vision of the future for museums is symptomatic of the vulnerability of a post-Trump American cultural sector anxious to secure its long-term sustainability in the wake of diminishing public funding, increasing competition for private sponsorship and mounting job insecurity among museum professionals. But regardless of its desirability or otherwise, it is a vision that is already beginning to take shape.

In Australia, decades of gradual divestment by national and state governments in cultural funding has generated ongoing downward pressure on staffing and budgets (van Barnefeld and Chiu 2017), forcing major libraries, museums and galleries to re-evaluate basic programs in order to meet mandated 'efficiency dividends'; while the small museum sector has been labelled a 'cultural ghetto of poverty and entrenched disadvantage' (Taylor 2016). Following a similar cultural policy trajectory through a period of financial austerity and public sector reforms,[1] museums in the United Kingdom have increasingly sought to demonstrate their public value by gesturing to their outward public service role, foregrounding contributions to urban renewal, tourism, local employment and life-long learning in preference to so-called 'intrinsic' cultural values that evade quantitative metrics.

Now thoroughly entangled in neoliberal productivity narratives and instrumentalist policy agendas, museums in the United States, United Kingdom, Australia and beyond must demonstrate accountability and return on public investment through entrepreneurial income generation and public programs that identifiably support communities and local economies in myriad ways. And, although cultural policy that uses funding as a reward for demonstrated performance against impact targets set by government has been criticised as market-driven cultural utilitarianism, this paradigm still informs the evaluation of cultural organisations (Scott 2015). In this context, the idea of hybridised collecting institutions, converged physically and digitally across disciplinary boundaries, has emerged as an administrative model for cultural provision that simultaneously hits accessibility, social impact and efficiency benchmarks.[2]

The establishment of the US Government's Institute for Museums and Library Services (IMLS) in 1996, the UK's Museums, Libraries and Archives Council (MLA) in 2000 and the Collections Council of Australia (CCA) in 2004 signalled accelerating momentum towards cross-domain collaboration worldwide at the beginning of the twenty-first century. In 2007, *RBM: A Journal of Rare Books, Manuscripts, and Cultural Heritage* (USA) devoted an entire issue to increasing collaboration and convergence across libraries, archives and museums. The coordinated publication in 2009 of special issues on digital convergence in *Library Quarterly*, *Archival Science* and *Museum Management and Curatorship* – all prominent academic journals – reinforced the significance of convergence within professional and academic discourse. In Australia, it has been proposed that the prevalence of collaboration and convergence justifies recognising GLAM (galleries, libraries, archives and museums) as a distinct and integrated discipline (Davis and Howard 2013), signalling the need for scholarship to define the theoretical scope of GLAM as a field of inquiry, as well as supporting the development of tailored higher-education training and best practice models. Rapid advancements in digital technologies continue to act as the catalyst for new initiatives to provide standardised and integrated access to collection databases, propelling forward discussions about brick-and-mortar convergence.

GLAM convergence also has a strong cultural policy and bureaucratic dimension. As governments in Europe and beyond have moved towards greater decentralisation and privatisation of cultural institutions (Boylan 2006), convergence of cognate organisations, such as libraries, archives and museums, has come to the fore as a policy solution to achieving financial rationalisation of cultural services. Likewise, in Australia, excitement around convergence has focussed on the promise of both financial and service delivery benefits: economies of scale, shared staffing and organisational structures, urban revitalisation and new audiences. Accelerating digital capacity has spurred initiatives to integrate access to distributed cultural collections via online portals like Europeana and Australia's Trove, aggregating the content of libraries and archives together with museums under the dual aims of universal access to information and institutional visibility. Since the early 2000s, various collaborations and physical amalgamations of museums, libraries, galleries and archives have emerged, governed by new funding and management models and a conceptual framework that promises to deliver greater productivity, sustainability and public participation.

But these shifts have also begun to challenge fundamental, long-held assumptions about the nature of museums, still encapsulated within the International Council of Museums' definition, in which collections and their interpretation play a pivotal role.[3] As museums continue to be transformed by the economic, policy and social forces shaping our world, what is the role of museum collections, and the processes through which knowledge is derived from and through them, in a hybridised institutional environment?

4 *Introduction*

How can we evaluate the impact of collections convergence on how meaning is created around objects? Can better understanding of changes to collection and curatorial practice in early experiments in convergence – where mergers have mostly been contained to organisations already classed as part of the GLAM sector – help us to navigate the potentially profound metamorphosis of the museum forecast for the not-too-distant future? And, when we talk about sustainability in the collections sector, is there an argument to be made for including 'interpretive sustainability' – the capacity for collecting institutions to preserve, develop and enact interpretive collection practices – within the debate?

Exploring these questions is the purpose of this book. By shining a spotlight on processes of collection interpretation at three case study institutions, *Interpreting Objects in the Hybrid Museum* engages with the phenomenon of convergence as an under-theorised bureaucratic model for structural change with unknown consequences for collection-focussed museum work. Drawing on an established lineage of theories about object interpretation in museums,[4] it contributes to the creation of a new, robust intellectual discourse around convergence, building a bridge between theory and practice and bringing to light fundamental questions regarding engagement with museum collections in a hybrid organisational context.

Internationally, cultural policy debates are often characterised by acrimonious and ultimately counterproductive polemics in which advocates for the intrinsic yet supposedly ineffable benefits of cultural activity are pit against an economic paradigm where the social contributions made by arts and culture – the so-called 'positive externalities' (Ruis-Ulldemolins 2016) – are framed quantitatively, and narrowly, through cost-benefit and return on investment analyses. This book seeks an alternative dialogue that moves beyond these dichotomies. By exploring convergence as not only a managerial but also an epistemic infrastructure for engaging with collections, the research highlights the impact of public policy (community service provision, local governance) on professional museum practice that, in turn, directly shapes the potential for knowledge creation and cultural production in the museum context. Testing the validity of commonly held assumptions about the intellectual and administrative benefits of cross-disciplinary, hybridised collection practice, it provides a 'street-level,' in-depth account of the often undocumented lived experiences of collection workers and the ways in which they translate organisational goals into operational realities.[5] In the absence of an established operational blueprint for convergence, this book exposes the institutional dynamics of hybrid organisations, examining the consequences of reconfigured domain boundaries and job descriptions for specialist museum activities and, ultimately, the potential for

Introduction 5

hybridisation to reshape fundamental understandings of identity, place, heritage and culture.

How the book works

Across the following chapters, *Interpreting Objects in the Hybrid Museum* examines the impact of hybridisation of museums with a dual focus on theories of meaning-making in museums and the ways in which related processes are activated within professional practice.

1 GLAM convergence: genealogy of a concept

This chapter establishes the contemporary context for the discussion, providing an overview of cultural policy issues, scholarship and professional literature dealing with convergence and outlining prevailing expectations around the cultural and community benefits of integrated collecting institutions.

There are both pragmatic and conceptual motivations driving the integration of museums, libraries and archives. Some commentaries point to the common ancestry of the collecting domains, insisting that the different types of repositories are inherently compatible, and current trends towards convergence are merely the fulfilment of historical precedents. Many authors justify convergence in reference to the new digital capacity to integrate access to collections online, eliminating the need for the now antiquated separation of the collecting domains and underscoring the timeliness of physical institutional convergence. In parallel, significant policy developments, including the decentralisation of cultural policy and the corresponding increased role of municipal councils in provision of cultural services (coupled with concerns about financial sustainability and return on taxpayer investment), serve as precursors to the advent of hybridisation as a model for development and management of new kinds of cultural facilities. Providing an overview of these intersecting trends, the chapter highlights prevailing assumptions about the benefits of convergence and outlines the potential of combining theory with fieldwork to critically examine the impacts of convergence 'on the ground' for interpretative museum practice.

2 Same same but different: rhetorics of knowledge in the convergence debate

Going to the conceptual heart of the convergence debate, Chapter 2 questions the impact of convergence on the creation of knowledge and meaning around collections. Contemporary hybridisation of the collecting domains is often justified on the basis that museums, libraries, archives and galleries are all 'knowledge institutions' or 'memory institutions,' implying that there is no substantial distinction (other than types of content) between the collecting domains. The argument follows that maintaining disciplinary boundaries only perpetuates redundant silos. But how do the different domains function to support the creation of knowledge, and are these processes compatible within blended organisations?

Chapter 2 explores this question by presenting an overview of discipline-specific ideas about how data, information and knowledge circulate and are produced through engagement with collections. I argue that, rather than revealing an essential affiliation between museums, libraries and archives, conflating them generically as knowledge institutions over-simplifies important differences in cataloguing, description, interpretation and deployment of collections. These differences lead museums, libraries and archives to engage with history, meaning and heritage in significantly diverse ways, producing a kaleidoscope of potential cultural encounters for end users of collections. The chapter troubles the claim that convergence will automatically deliver greater knowledge to these users, or necessarily enrich their interactions with collections, setting up the next chapter to assess how these issues play out in practice within converged institutions.

3 Process conflict: interpreting museum collections within the convergence context

As the first of two chapters focussing on the findings of the fieldwork, Chapter 3 looks at the influence of convergence on areas of museum practice specifically related to the development, management and presentation of museum collections. Drawing on staff interviews at three cultural institutions, each representing a distinct model of convergence or hybridisation, I focus on thematic connections across cases that speak directly to the capacity (or not) of collection workers to engage with collections in ways that produce meaningful and rich understandings of their cultural significance.

The findings are grouped around three distinct but interconnected themes – collections, exhibitions and interpretation – through which I explore the ability of staff to perform tasks related to acquisitions and collection development, documentation and description, preservation and development of permanent and temporary exhibitions. Building on the preceding chapter, the findings are examined in reference to the different interpretive approaches existing within the library, archives, visual arts and museum professions. I explore how these methods interact, and sometimes clash, in converged institutional settings and discuss the implications for knowledge creation around museum collections.

4 Mixed messages: organisational structure and management of convergence

Having looked at how practices of museum interpretation are carried out in converged institutions by staff responsible for collections, this chapter considers the impact of high-level administrative changes brought on by convergence, asking whether newly implemented policy and bureaucratic changes also have a flow-on effect on collection-level work. I consider how administration, funding and organisational structure, together with the strategic goals and leadership of a converged organisation, can impact on the ways in which collections are documented, researched and presented to visitors.

Extending ideas presented in the previous chapter, the staff interviews demonstrate how the broad management frameworks of convergence produce particular conditions for museum practice. The allocation of resources, expectations regarding staff collaboration and the redesign of individual job descriptions combine in interesting ways to dictate both the extent and context of staff engagement with objects, with surprising consequences for their ability to explore the meanings of collections.

Conclusion: Interpretive sustainability in the hybrid institution

Bringing together and comparing the philosophy and practice of convergence, this concluding chapter presents a realistic and evidence-based assessment of the capacity of hybrid collecting institutions to enrich our understanding of the cultural materials they hold. Contrary to the optimism surrounding the 'first wave' of convergence represented by the case studies, I show how management structures and everyday barriers to interpretive practice can conspire to impede both physical and intellectual access to collections, producing institutions that achieve, from a meaning-making perspective, potentially less than the sum of their individual parts.

What do these insights mean for future iterations of the convergence concept, as the sustainability of individual collecting institutions continues to be threatened by increasing economic and often political pressures? What aspects of museum provision can be productively hybridised, and which elements of disciplinary specialisation need to be protected so that we can retain and enhance our engagement with important cultural collections? This chapter culminates with a range of suggestions for organisational design and management, providing a timely evidence-based intervention into a rapidly evolving sphere of cultural policy.

Interpreting Objects in the Hybrid Museum responds to an identified lack of museum studies literature that engages directly with museums as a field of practice realised, and continually (re)produced, through the daily

8 *Introduction*

experiences, decisions and actions of museum workers.[6] Underpinning this project is the notion of the museum as a 'process' that is in a perpetual state of becoming through the interplay of organisational policies and dynamics, institutional history, discipline-based practices (research, interpretation, collection care and management) and various kinds of engagements with visitors and stakeholders. This book is therefore intended as both a theory-driven provocation and a fieldwork analysis that aims to widen the discourse between museological scholarship and cultural policy-making, with relevance to government stakeholders, museum administrators and professional museum workers. The book presents richly detailed first-hand accounts of museum work embedded in hybridised collecting institutions in order to dismantle the perceived gulf between theory and practice and provide insights grounded in everyday collection work that can be readily assimilated back into institutional planning.

In acknowledgement of the limitations of a short book format, *Interpreting Objects in the Hybrid Museum* consciously and unapologetically focusses on the creation of meaning around collections at the level of professional museum practice, performed by staff trained in this disciplinary field. Although beyond the scope of this volume, emerging approaches to participatory museology that engage with theories of cultural democracy,[7] as well as an increasing museological focus on materiality and wider theories of affect,[8] represent equally important perspectives on how collections are understood in museum contexts. This book approaches museum interpretive practice as one generative element that contributes to the epistemic and phenomenological assemblage constituting meaningful museum experience. In acknowledgement of the expanding horizon of museological research, a judicious, holistic and longitudinal analysis of the multiple dimensions of meaning formation around collections will be essential to realising a future vision of hybridised collections capable of sustaining the culturally enriching encounters that make museums distinctive and worthwhile.

Notes

1 For an extended analysis, see Gray 2002 and 2017.
2 The trend for collaboration across collecting domains now extends to Africa, where a recent study (Saurombe and Ngulube 2016) conducted by the East and Southern Africa Regional Branch of the International Council on Archives (ESARBICA) recommended that archives could extend their visibility and social impact by improving public programming through collaboration with museums and libraries.
3 The current ICOM Statutes, adopted in Vienna on August 24, 2007, provide the following definition of a museum: 'A museum is a non-profit, permanent institution in the service of society and its development, open to the public, which acquires, conserves, researches, communicates and exhibits the tangible and

Introduction 9

intangible heritage of humanity and its environment for the purposes of education, study and enjoyment.'

4 Notable contributions include compendiums by Lubar and Kingery (1993), Schlereth (1982) and Pearce (1994) and, more recently, work by Bal (2004) and Carr (2006) and Crane (2011).

5 In a study conducted over the same period as the research for this book, the UK Arts and Humanities Research Council's Cultural Value Project employed a similar methodology to 'break down the divide between the intrinsic and instrumental [cultural policy] camps' (Crossick and Kaszynska 2016, 5). This research aligns with Michael Lipksy's influential approach to understanding public policy delivery through the lens of 'street-level' bureaucracy.

6 For a discussion of the importance of museum studies research that is grounded in the actual practices and experiences of museum workers, see Conal McCarthy's introduction to the *Museum Practice* volume of the International Handbooks of Museum Studies (2015).

7 In the last decade, building on momentum generated through the 'New Museology' movement of the 1980s and 1990s, a variety of professional and scholarly debates about audience engagement and inclusion have coalesced into a distinct museological discourse about participation that traverses a range of related themes, including multivocality and shared authority in museum practice (e.g. Heumann Gurian 2010; Simon 2010; Savage-Yamakazi and Murrell 2015), the social justice obligation of museums (e.g. Lynch and Alberti 2010; Golding and Modest 2013; Paquet Kinsley 2016) and community self-representation (e.g. Onciul 2013; Hutchison 2013).

8 Discussions about phenomenological encounter, material agency, sensory interaction and the role of affective experience in the creation of knowledge around museum collections and heritage include Sandra Dudley's edited compilation *Museum Materialities* (2010) but also more specific case studies such as those by Byrne (2013) and Golanska (2015).

1 GLAM convergence
Genealogy of a concept

> *To me, we will eventually ... see that you can tell the story of humanity through all of its objects, all presented together, complex and dynamic in narrative.*
>
> —manager of Westlands

What is convergence anyway?

Reflecting the fluidity of the convergence model and the variety of converged institutions that have come into being, a strong and binding definition of 'convergence' remains elusive. The blanket usage of the term conceals the diversity of institutional partnerships, mergers and restructures it is used to describe. Converged or hybrid institutions differ considerably at the level of sharing and collaboration between the constituent organisations. There appears to be no consensus surrounding the explicit meaning of the term and what exactly it entails for the design of staff roles, institutional missions and public programs.

In the international scene, there has been an attempt to define the meaning of convergence with greater precision. In 2001, Christopher Marsden of the V&A Museum Archives referred to the concept as 'integration,' describing it as 'one of the chief concerns of the moment for the archive profession' (Marsden 2001, 17). Marsden distinguished different forms of convergence in terms of 'institutional integration,' where organisations are physically combined, and 'macro-integration,' where organisations remain autonomous but cooperate on joint development of products and services. In 2007, the British librarian and scholar Gerald Beasley observed the emergence of two main trends or modes of convergence between libraries, archives and museums. The first involved greater collaboration between the

GLAM convergence 11

domains, especially in the digital and online spheres, characterised by the hybridisation of collection information, which would become 'more open to being shared, transferred, sliced and diced' (Beasley 2007, 21). The second trend involved the actual organisational amalgamation of institutions. In this sense, *digital* convergence, which hinges on information sharing via the standardisation of metadata across digital collection records and interoperable database technology, is quite distinct from *physical* convergence, where the integration and cross-pollination of previously independent collections have the potential to bring about a profound and permanent alteration in their constitution and subsequent interpretation.

In 2008, research on university collections in the USA and UK – published under the cheeky title *Beyond the Silos of the LAMs: Collaboration Among Libraries, Archives and Museums* – described increasing cooperation between collecting organisations as an incremental 'collaboration continuum' (Zorich, Waibel and Erway 2008). The research defined convergence as an endpoint where collaboration 'mature[s] to the level of infrastructure and becomes, like our water transportation networks, a critical system that we rely upon without considering the collaborative efforts and compromises that made it possible' (Zorich, Waibel and Erway 2008, 12). To put it another way, genuine convergence is a situation where organisations become integrated and mutually reliant to a point where they can no longer function as autonomous units. Bastian and Harvey (2012) elaborated the model by identifying three key facets of convergence: the co-existence and integration of different kinds of collection documentation, the formulation of common information management practices and the leveraging of traditional, domain-based processes towards the development of innovative cultural programs and services:

> A converging cultural heritage institution is one that combines library, archival and museum material, and is working towards a set of standards and best practices that unites traditional theory and operations from each.
> (Bastian and Harvey 2012, 2–3)

In the absence of a definitive conceptual or operational model, these various attempts to characterise convergence are perhaps more useful in outlining what it is *not*. Convergence does not simply describe a positive inclination towards cooperation or collaboration between GLAMs in the delivery of occasional projects and public programs. It is not mere co-location of facilities in cultural precincts or otherwise autonomous organisations in shared buildings. Rather, it denotes a more fundamental hybridisation of professional and disciplinary practices that crystallises into a new

12 GLAM convergence

operational entity – either in the form of digital information architecture or organisational structures or physical collection spaces – that cannot be easily categorised according to conventional domain boundaries from a user's perspective.[1] Convergence, at least ideally, should generate new ways of working with, and experiences of, cultural collections that amount to more than the sum of their GLAM parts.

The persisting ambiguity around the definition of convergence, together with its anticipated benefits, represents a fertile opportunity for research that can immediately be applied to the evolving academic, professional and public policy discourses around the topic. As a first step, this chapter maps the genesis of contemporary notions of convergence to discern the underlying expectations surrounding hybridised GLAMs, including improved user access, integrated experiences and richer understandings of collections, administrative efficiencies and the wider contribution to public policy that convergence is supposed to deliver. Understanding the motivations behind convergence establishes a baseline against which the trend is investigated at both the theoretical and empirical level in the subsequent chapters of this book.

The historical precedent argument

Contemporary arguments for the convergence of collecting domains are often predicated on the common ancestry of libraries, archives and museums. From this perspective, collaboration and hybridisation across institutions simply represent the reunification of collections that traditionally belong together, righting an accident of history that saw museums, libraries and archives develop as independent spheres of professional practice in spite of their aligned content.

Writing in 2007 as Director of the IMLS (Institute of Museums and Library Services, USA),[2] Robert Martin pointed to the shared history of libraries, archives and museums, referencing the ancient library of Alexandria (also called the Mouseion, or Temple of the Muses), destroyed in 48 BCE, as the archetypal 'converged' collecting institution.[3] Others contend that the integration of libraries, archives and museums is a return to an earlier mode of collecting developed in the sixteenth century in Europe, where wealthy 'gentlemen scholars' assembled collections of books, documents, specimens and artefacts in microcosmic cabinets of curiosities.[4]

Museologist Eileen Hooper-Greenhill has noted that the birth of the Modern period in nineteenth century Europe was marked by the desire to reinvent knowledge as a purely rational pursuit, attempting to 'cut away those aspects of knowledge that were seen as superstitious, subjective, emotive, and ultimately, unreasonable' (2000, 105). The meaning of artefacts in collections came to be seen as concrete, fixed and unambiguous, allowing objects to be 'read' like books and supporting the common educational goal of museums and libraries (Given and McTavish 2010; Gibson, Morris and Cleeve 2007). Within this paradigm, collections of books, documents and artefact collections could be seen as inherently compatible. Every kind of object was a source of objective information, and, when organised together according to a subject area such as natural history, collections could create a reservoir of tangible, observable and readable knowledge on a particular theme.

Analysis provided by a number of other authors – some of whom happen to be proponents of convergence – indicates that there are historical justifications for the autonomous existence of libraries, archives and museums. Given and McTavish (2010) argue that the professionalisation of libraries, archives and museums in the beginning of the twentieth century meant increasing specialisation around the documentation and presentation of different collection types, diminishing the practicality and conceptual appropriateness of dealing jointly with collections. In the USA and Canada, for example, systematic library education became formalised around 1920,[5] with programs for museum professionals to follow during the 1930s. Likewise, the growth of librarianship as a profession, and the accompanying need to develop more efficient systems for dealing with expanding collections of books and journals, contributed to the separation of printed collections from other forms of material culture (Beasley 2007).

In the USA during the 1950s and 1960s, standardisation across library collection documentation and management was advanced with the application of computing technology to library cataloguing, leading to the development of the machine-readable cataloguing (MARC) format, which was adopted nationally in 1971 (Hedstrom and King 2004). This development, alongside similar attempts to standardise library classification and cataloguing rules in Britain and Europe, precipitated the publication of the International Standard Bibliographic Description (ISBD) by the International Federation of Library Associations (IFLA) during the early 1970s, with refinements and extensions to the standard continuing until today (Byrum 1997; Hedstrom and King 2004). As Hedstrom and King point out, these classification procedures imposed a particular epistemological framework – an 'epistemic infrastructure' – on library collections worldwide, based on the ideals of encyclopaedism and scientific rationalism (2004, 18). The emphasis placed on achieving ubiquitous cataloguing protocols across libraries – with the aim of streamlining their philosophical frameworks, collection description methods and the physical order of bibliographic collections – contributed to positioning librarianship as a consolidated professional field requiring highly specialised training.

14 *GLAM convergence*

Evolving in tandem with the library field, museum practice and theory have nevertheless developed along a trajectory that acknowledges non-standardised classification schemes, heterogeneous approaches to object interpretation, a wide variety of material culture expertise and an emphasis on mediated public access to collections. A considerable body of literature exists around the topic of object interpretation in museums, with many approaches published during the 1980s and 1990s in a number of seminal edited museological publications (e.g. Schlereth 1982; Pearce 1994; Lubar and Kingery 1993). The different methodologies for artefact study anthologised in these volumes exemplify the influence of diverse disciplinary approaches and epistemological perspectives underpinning different museums.

Archives present yet another model of collecting, often viewed first and foremost in their role of preserving information contained in unique records, rather than as overt interpreters of content. The idea of the archive was conceived around the principle of preservation of documentary materials, later evolving an official bureaucratic function (Featherstone 2006). Archives provided 'raw' content that could be mined and interpreted by scholars, governments and other external users for legal, administrative or historiographic purposes. In contrast, especially to museums, interpretation of collection holdings in historical or thematic contexts by archivists is still discouraged and even regarded as antithetical to good archival practice, as aptly expressed in the following extract from a widely used Australian manual of archival practice:

> Archives have many potential uses and an archivist cannot know exactly what these uses may be in the future. Rather than rearranging records in a way that might be 'useful' to a particular audience, archivists preserve the original order so that records can be understood in their original context, giving room for users to interpret and analyse the records in a multitude of ways.
>
> (Bettington et al. 2008, 18)

The primary concerns of archives lie in retaining the relationship between the documents and the institutional and personal functions and activities that gave rise to them. Correspondingly, archival records are arranged and described in series, rather than as individual items. Ideally, each user follows their own path through the order of the archive, making their own sense of the collection without the inference of any pre-imposed understanding. In a neat analogy, archives have been described as 'wholesalers' that provide raw research materials for others to interpret, while museums can be seen as 'retailers' with ready-made products (exhibitions, public programs and other forms of communication) for their users (Yakel 2005, 16).

This brief overview of the collecting domains demonstrates that important differences exist in the perceived purpose and arrangement of different types of collections. The content and organisation of library, archive and museum holdings are a reflection of different institutional missions, traditions in collection management and control and perceptions of object value (Dempsey 2000). Each domain enacts its own legal processes, visitor access rules, loan policies, conservation strategies, object disposal procedures and other collection management approaches that can produce vastly different outcomes for relatively similar collection items (Robison 2007). Increasing professionalisation in the collections sector continues to be an important factor in the development of libraries, archives and museums as distinct collecting domains, complicating the argument for convergence in regard to appropriate professional training.

Nonetheless, much of the scholarship in support of GLAM convergence and hybridisation persists with the view that there is a purely typological difference between the published material collected by libraries, the government and institutional records collected by archives and the individual objects collected by museums. This 'artificial distinction' creates an unnecessary barrier for users, who are obliged to search across repositories in order to gather together diverse materials required for their research, educational needs and other purposes.[6] From this point of view, it is easy to envisage the benefits of digital or physical convergence in streamlining access to collection resources and making the use of collections less cumbersome. Rooted in an empiricist epistemology (to which I will return in the next chapter), the typological differences between collections become irrelevant, rendering both physical and intellectual obstacles to the joint management and provision of collections obsolete.

New technologies and the 'virtual Wunderkammer'

Rapid innovation in digital technologies and growing demand for broadly accessible learning resources have added considerable momentum to discussion about GLAM collaboration, with the aim of developing aggregated collection information and converged web-based collection platforms.[7] With the advent of online collection databases, Robert Martin (2007) argued that the conventional separation of library, archive and museum information would no longer be tolerated by users, who do 'not care whether the original materials are in a library or a museum or an archives. . . . They just want access to "the stuff"' (Martin 2007, 82). He proposed that domain-specific conventions for collection documentation were counterproductive, especially where users were becoming accustomed to unhindered access to other kinds of information via the internet. The implication is that technological breakthroughs and universal online connectivity would facilitate the release of vast reserves of knowledge around collections – knowledge that previously remained untapped by the majority of users before the arrival of the World Wide Web. Siloed professional practices, disciplinary distinctions and time-consuming processes that characterise 'physical' collecting institutions seem starkly at odds with the fluidity, ongoing rapid development, responsiveness and accessibility of digital technology.

Increasing competition for users' attention from private enterprises such as Google and Amazon, who have a commercial incentive to invest in cutting-edge database and user experience technologies, has simultaneously emerged as an existential threat to collecting institutions (Hedstrom and King 2004). A more cohesive, networked presence has been seen as vital to libraries, archives and museums 'securing their space in this colossal virtual *Wunderkammer*' (Waibel and Erway 2009, 325). Echoing this sentiment, in 2007, James Neal – vice president for information services and university librarian at Columbia University – referred to the need to manage the 'collective collection,' rather than individual library, archive and museum repositories, as well as 'renovating descriptive and organizing practices' to create common vocabularies and standards for collection management (Neal 2007, 266–67). The IMLS (2008) emphasised that the

> increased use of, and reliance on, digital resources has blurred traditional distinctions between organizations, prompting an increased focus on the shared information needs and challenges facing libraries, archives and museums in the information age.[8]

In this sense, digital convergence hinges on information sharing via the standardisation of metadata across digital collection records and interoperable database technology. The advancement of digital technology has not only raised the bar for provision of online collections access for all kinds of collecting institutions but also triggered questions about the long-term viability of operating separate collecting domains and physical collection spaces.

Financial and public policy imperatives

In concert with digital disruption and the perceived obsolescence of disciplinary silos, the quest for greater cost efficiency and long-term economic sustainability of cultural organisations has emerged as a powerful influence on convergence trends internationally. Research carried out between 2001 and 2003 (Boylan 2006) found that governments in Europe and around the world were rapidly moving away from taxpayer funding towards greater decentralisation and privatisation of cultural institutions, with the associated adoption of self-financing models.[9] Since the 1980s, reforms across the public sector in the UK (known as the 'new public management') have ushered in a growing emphasis on financial efficiency, target-setting and performance measurement (Taylor and Kelly 2006, 630). The introduction of competitive market economics into the UK public sector has seen declining central government support, higher emphasis on accountability to service end users (envisaged as 'clients' or 'customers') and a demand for publicly funded organisations to provide evidence of value for money in terms of their social impact. In the USA, the availability of funding to cultural organisations is also being restricted, with a variety of factors, including rising energy costs, diminishing local philanthropic support and the pervasive threat of economic downturn, projected to continue downward funding pressure on museums well into the twenty-first century (Chung, Wilkening and Johnstone 2008). In Australia, Canada and some European countries, the decentralisation of funding for cultural services has also seen already stretched local authorities become the primary funders of the small to medium museum and gallery sector, local libraries and a range of other cultural programs through a trend I call the 'municipalisation of culture' (Robinson 2018).

As early as 2001, UK archivist Christopher Marsden identified government policies and funding models biased towards the rationalisation of services as the primary driver of convergence of collecting institutions. In a similar policy context, US heritage consultant David Curry predicted that cultural organisations would increasingly look to convergence as a pathway to financial resilience in the face of economic stress (Curry 2010a). Michelle Doucet (2007), writing on the amalgamation of the National Library and National Archives in Canada in 2004, also cited shrinking resources, and the resulting need for greater scale and efficiency, as the rationale behind the merger of the two organisations.

In their summary of literature dealing with museum and library collaboration in England and the USA, Gibson, Morris and Cleeve (2007) identified the sharing of facilities and funding resources, as well as the possibility of rationalising costs, as some of the most pervasive grounds for convergence. Their research into collaborations between libraries and museums found that some organisations believe financial aid from funding agencies would be easier to obtain if they were seen to be working together. In the digital environment, De Laurentis (2006) proposed that libraries, archives and museums should see their collections as financial assets and exploit them to create products and obtain revenue even though this would require a shift away from the mindset that cultural organisations exist outside the economic realm and are purely for public benefit.

These views point to a changing perception of cultural collections away from a government-funded resource available to all to a commodity in the financial marketplace able to generate income to support ongoing operational requirements. Convergence is positioned as an efficiency model capable of delivering economies of scale, greater access to funding opportunities and improved visibility for cultural organisations. In various individual combinations, shifts in policy and the economic environment mean there is increasing pressure on national, state and local government-run collecting institutions to remain financially sustainable by operating with greater efficiency.

Indicators of this efficiency are not, however, limited to how well these organisations perform against their internal strategic objectives. Arts and culture have been instrumentalised through a process of 'attachment' to wider government economic and social programs (Gray 2002, 2017), which are deemed more critical than cultural provision to a society's overall wellbeing. Culture is seen as a tool – a means to an end – rather than representing value in and of itself. From this perspective, cultural institutions, including museums, libraries, galleries and archives, earn their keep by demonstrating that they contribute to a host of extrinsic government goals. On the one hand, they may be envisioned as 'creative industries' or 'entertainment businesses' (Mulcahy 2006) that support employment growth, technical innovation, national exports, urban revitalisation or tourism. Alternatively, they are co-opted in the service of social integration, community cohesion, mental health or life-long learning. When combined with restricted and ever-diminishing government funding, this expanded horizon of public accountabilities creates a challenging and potentially contradictory set of expectations for the GLAM sector that can be boiled down to the proverbial imperative to 'do more with less' (and to prove it). The swing towards self-generated income and efficiency also raises the question of whether the collection management, curatorial and public programs of hybrid GLAMs will be geared towards attaining profitability, eschewing experimental projects in favour of conservative, risk-averse or popular content that guarantees return on investment.

New museology and GLAM democratisation

Finally, even a shorthand review of factors contributing to the trend towards convergence and hybridisation of GLAMs would not be complete without considering the influence of the theoretical reorientation of museums embodied within the 'new' or 'critical' museology movement, which gained traction in English-speaking countries in the late twentieth century. Fashioned as a response to the exclusionary practices of the 'traditional' museum model that functioned to maintain 'the cultural hegemony of the elite' (Halpin 1997, 52), this movement rejected the unquestioned historical and scientific metanarratives that had, in the view of new museologists, too long been used to underwrite curatorial authority, justify passive acquiescence of audiences to museum-driven educational objectives and restrict museum professional training to technical concerns (see, for example, Stam 1993; Bennett 1995; Shelton 2013; McCall and Gray 2014). Responding instead to wider challenges to the museum as governmental institution through the lens of power relations in society, this new museology embraced critical evaluation of the museum as its modus operandi in a quest to democratise, decolonise and inject cultural diversity into all aspects of museum practice, but especially interpretation of collections and the design of public programs.

By 1999, the eminent American museologist and museum administrator Stephen Weil was writing that museums had shifted from 'being about something to being for somebody' (Weil 1999). Around the same time that contemporary convergences of museums with other types of collecting institutions were beginning to take place, Weil was identifying a significant recalibration of museums from inward-facing, operationally focussed institutions towards a social outcomes model of museum provision. Along with this transition came the imperative for museums to demonstrate their public value, which, according to Weil, could be measured according to two fundamental criteria: financial transparency and accountability and positive impacts on quality of life. The museum was becoming

> a transformed and redirected institution that can, through its public-service orientation, use its very special competencies in dealing with objects to contribute positively to the quality of individual human lives and to enhance the well-being of human communities.
>
> (Weil 1999, 231)

It is no wonder, then, that cultural policy developments in favour of convergence – driven by the prospect of increased economic efficiency (cost-cutting) and measurable return on investment in the form of cultural utilitarianism – have received relatively little criticism in the museological scholarship. In fact, the justification for efficiency measures, couched in rhetoric around the museum as a publicly accountable community service, dovetails smoothly with the democratising ethos characterising the 'new museology' movement that has continued to drive contemporary museum agendas for broad-based stakeholder inclusion, improved access to collections and social activism. The instrumentalist bent of this philosophy was built into the earliest articulations of new museological discourse. According to the Declaration of Quebec, the result of the First International Workshop on 'Ecomuseums and the New Museology' organised by ICOM[10] in 1984,

> the new museology – ecomuseology, community museology and all other forms of active museology – is primarily concerned with community development, reflecting the driving forces in social progress and associating them in its plans for the future.
>
> (Mayrand 2015, 116)

At its heart, museological critique since the early 1980s has moved towards deconstructing what it has regarded as rigid and authoritarian models of museum provision, reforming them according to a philosophy of social inclusion, grassroots relevance, stakeholder participation and provision of a 'public good.'

The term 'third place' has been used to describe the social function of museums, libraries and other cultural organisations as democratised sites for communal activities and civic engagement that combat the alienating effects of contemporary urban isolation. An online forum conducted in 2010 addressing this concept describes the third place as 'a neutral community space, where people come together voluntarily and informally in ways that level social iniquities and promote community engagement and social connection' (Hildreth 2010). In Australia, the NSW Library Council's *Bookends Scenarios* report observed that the growing number of people living alone, as well as increased urbanisation, has elevated the community-building role of libraries as a secure and accessible third place for people to socialise (Freeman and Watson 2009, 12, 53, 56). Similarly, Public Libraries NSW highlighted the beneficial role of libraries in providing a welcoming and safe public meeting space (Don 2008, 2; see also Baum 2008). Research by the IMLS (Griffiths and King 2008) highlights the high level of trust placed in museums and libraries by public users – a quality that enables them to act as sites for safe and meaningful social interaction (Weil 1999; Wright 2010). Similar ideas have been prominent in broader museum, library and archive discourses surrounding how collecting institutions can engage and connect with communities and better respond to the needs of their constituents (Gomez 2010), prompting calls for greater collaboration between the collecting domains.

In the UK, research conducted in 2007 focussing on collaborative projects between libraries and museums in the UK and USA revealed 'the encouragement of community development through social inclusion was an important motivating force in a number of collaborative projects' (Gibson, Morris and Cleeve 2007, 60). The targeting of a similar range of visitor demographic groups by both libraries and museums – including children and teenagers, people from non–English-speaking backgrounds, those taking part in continuing education, teachers and researchers – was seen as justification for cooperation between institutions. In this context, museums in particular are seen to have a two-fold responsibility to act as facilitators for communities to articulate and engage with significant cultural themes (Sola 1997; Carr 2006; Patchen 2006; Chinn 2010) and to use museum expertise in converged settings to identify and foreground issues of emerging social importance. Furthermore, the renewed emphasis in the museum sector on education and public programs since the 1980s (Genoways 2006) has aligned museums more closely with the social purpose of libraries.

GLAM convergence: a confluence of historical, technological, policy and conceptual trends

The contemporary movement towards hybridisation and convergence of different kinds of collections and collecting practices can itself be understood as the product of a broader confluence of a number of factors, each of which has acted independently as a catalyst in the spheres of museology, digital innovation and cultural policy development. I have outlined the historical precedent argument, which points to the common ancestry of libraries, museums and archives as evidence of the redundancy of separate collecting institutions. Insisting that the different types of repositories are inherently compatible, current trends towards convergence are merely the fulfilment of a historical precedent. After all, they all collect 'stuff' and all that stuff is in some way 'cultural,' right? Does it really make sense, then, to maintain separate repositories when the users of that cultural material no longer care where it is housed?

Highlighting the common ancestry of GLAMs gains further traction in the light of the second catalyst for convergence: the exponential advancement of digital information and communication technologies over the last three decades. Never before has the potential existed for the cultural patrimony of humankind, sequestered for so long in the siloed stores of museums, libraries and archives, to be released, recombined and made accessible to anyone via interoperable digital collection databases and online curatorial programs. New digital technologies offer unprecedented capacity to integrate users' access to collections online, eliminating the need for 'antiquated' separation of the collecting domains and underscoring the timeliness of physical institutional convergence. And the possibility of simultaneously achieving near universal, democratised access to cultural material and rationalisation of services is an irresistible lure to governments pursuing public sector reform, lower spending and impact-driven return on taxpayer investment. Finally, the democratising, reflexive, public service orientation of the 'new museology' has provided a common platform for the objectives of GLAMs as cognate, user-driven organisations, easily aligning their objectives with the instrumentalist demands of financial efficiency and public sector reform. The joint perception of collecting institutions as 'third places' has refocussed attention away from typological differences between collections. Emphasis on the wider social role of GLAMs, their programs and the community spaces they offer provides further impetus to the idea of convergence.

It all sounds too good to be true, except that there's an unacknowledged complication in the first assumption underpinning this utopian vision.

The conflation of GLAMs within the hybridised convergence model fundamentally rejects the understanding of museums (and, indeed, libraries, archives and galleries) as sites for particular meaning-making practices, instead reducing them to passive warehouses of cultural objects. The interpretive role of museums is absent from this vision. Collections are thought of simply as 'raw content' to which end users should be granted unfettered access, able (and entitled) to make their own sense of the material. Disciplinary distinctions between GLAMs – which are essentially different contexts for understanding what collections mean and how they can be useful – are invisible to this critique. As a result, any obstacles to hybridisation and convergence are reduced to merely technical and logistic issues.

In this context, museums and collections are understood as tangible assets, rather than interpretive spheres. They are seen as 'things,' rather than arenas of particular kinds of cultural practice – their value situated in their nominal presence and inventory. There is no connection made between the extrinsic benefits of museums (predominantly output-driven ideas of value based on economic and social multiplier effects) and how it is that museums actually generate these outcomes. This leads to reductive quantitative performance indicators that privilege product over process (e.g. number of exhibitions or events, rather than quality, source or participant engagement). Integration with other kinds of cultural institutions is therefore narrowly construed in terms of the consolidation of assets, predominantly in the context of decreasing expenditure.

While GLAMs all collect, and their collections are indeed cultural, it is what happens after objects cross the thresholds of these different domains that distinguishes their purpose and meaningfulness. In the next chapter, I problematise the easy conflation of GLAMs along historical, technological and policy lines. I suggest that greater attention to the information

GLAM convergence 23

and knowledge potential of collections, born of the particular interpretive traditions of museums, libraries, archives and galleries, is fundamental to understanding the relationship between these domains and therefore a necessary precursor to their potentially successful integration.

Notes

1 It is important to acknowledge that different kinds of repositories have long co-existed within collecting organisations. For example, most state and national museums in Australia, and indeed around the world, retain their own archival and library collections. However, it is important to distinguish between these examples – where the archives and library play a supporting role serving the identity and activities of the museum as the dominant partner – and recent examples of the supposedly non-hierarchical 'convergence' of previously autonomous collecting institutions.
2 The IMLS is also the principal federal funding body for libraries and museums in the USA.
3 Much like modern-day universities, the Mouseion was a repository of books, documents and objects, as well as a centre of scholarship.
4 See Weil 1999; Waibel and Erway 2009; Given and McTavish 2010; Madsen 2010; Bickersteth 2010; Hedstrom and King 2004.
5 Hjorland notes that a Department of Library Science existed in Chicago as early as 1894 (Hjorland 2000, 27).
6 For example, see Tanackovic and Badurina 2009.
7 See Dempsey 2000; De Laurentis 2006; Doucet 2007; Neal 2007; Zorich, Waibel and Erway 2008; Waibel and Erway 2009; Duff et al. 2013.
8 Institute of Museum and Library Services (IMLS) and Florida State University 2008:1.
9 See also Hedstrom and King 2004; Genoways 2006.
10 International Council of Museums.

2 Same same but different
Rhetorics of knowledge in the convergence debate

> *The museum curator or education officer or collection manager will . . . read the catalogue information and add to the information by fleshing out the understanding of it in an interpretive way.*
>
> —former director, national collections sector agency

GLAMs are frequently described as 'knowledge institutions,' with the assumption that a shared interest in the diffusion of knowledge through society justifies their integration. Within this discourse, physical access to collections correlates with intellectual access, and there is an implied equivalence between the possession of information – regardless of its source – and that of knowledge acquisition. Yet the mechanics of knowledge production in the context of converged collections remains to be described. How is knowledge created in museums, libraries and archives? Is it the same kind of knowledge? How important is it to maintain the different knowledge 'products' of GLAMs? If it turns out that different processes for the creation of knowledge are valuable, can these processes withstand inevitable recalibration through GLAM hybridisation and convergence?

The reductive historical, technological and cultural policy arguments for convergence outlined in the previous chapter offer no easy answers to these questions. To understand how hybridised institutional structures might alter established GLAM approaches to produce new kinds of knowledge around collections, we need to consider the problem first through a conceptual lens.

The first task of this chapter is to establish the prevalent understanding of the term 'knowledge' within the discourse around convergence, mapping how the creation and exchange of knowledge around collections is used as a rationale for hybridisation of GLAMs. I then apply an epistemological

Same same but different 25

evaluation of these assumed benefits by examining the sources, structure and parameters of 'knowledge' in relation to various types of collections. Theorists in the fields of museology, archives theory, library and information science have proposed different ways of understanding the related concepts of data, information and knowledge across museums, libraries and archives. Any conceptual framework for convergence needs to take into account how these ideas might interact in a hybridised collections context. In other words, what does it mean to 'know' something about an object in a museum, as compared to a library or archive? How is that 'knowledge' recorded and communicated? A closer examination of the museum context is used to elaborate ways in which specific epistemological frameworks can develop around collections by interpreting them through the lens of a particular kind of institution.

Having identified the theoretical reference points, it is possible to evaluate the appropriateness of the idea of 'knowledge institutions' against the empirical evidence presented in the chapters to follow. This chapter sets up what is intellectually at stake in the convergence debate. Understanding how collecting institutions come to 'know' their collections through various processes of interpretation is critical in the design of physically or digitally integrated services. Are domain-specific approaches to collection knowledge compatible and easily transferable between the collecting domains? By plotting a range of possible knowledge engagements with collections, the importance of including 'interpretive sustainability' as a criterion in the future planning of converged collection spaces emerges.

Converged collecting organisations as 'Knowledge Institutions'

Literature in support of both the physical and digital convergence of library, archive and museum collections reveals the centrality of the concept of 'knowledge' in legitimising the trend. The novelty and appeal of contemporary models of convergence in the collections sector are linked to the promise of improved opportunities for knowledge acquisition, and this relationship is readily apparent in the language used to describe such models. In their paper considering the history of the convergence trend, Given and McTavish cited Ian Wilson, then the librarian and archivist of Canada, who described the 2004 integration of Libraries and Archives Canada as revolutionary because the organisation represented 'a new kind of knowledge institution' (Given and McTavish 2010, 7). Similarly, as the title of their paper suggests, Kirchoff, Schweibenz and Sieglerschmidt (2008) describe the digital convergence of library, archive and museum collections in Germany, through the development of the joint BAM Internet portal, as motivated by 'the spell of ubiquitous knowledge'. They cite extensively from Lorcan Dempsey's influential 2000 paper that emphasised the benefit of convergence in creating 'knowledge networks' (Dempsey 2000, 3). Likewise, Waibel and Erway outline the potential of digital convergence to revive the ideal of a 'deeply interconnected LAM [library, archive and museum] knowledgebase' (Waibel and Erway 2009, 325). Within a similar context, libraries, archives and museums have been described interchangeably as 'physical knowledge exchanges' (Dempsey 2000, 3), the 'knowledge industry' (Enser 2001, 428), 'knowledge centres' (Macnaught 2008) and 'knowledge domains' (CILIP 2009) with a shared mission of 'knowledge transfer within society' (Enser 2001, 424).

As these examples show, much of the discourse in support of convergence is underscored by the assumption that more knowledge – presumably for users – will automatically be generated via integration of the collecting domains. Ideally, GLAM hybridisation promises democratised and universal access to information and knowledge, fostering deeper engagement with all forms of cultural heritage.

The influence of digital technologies

Digital technologies and the internet present unprecedented possibilities for integration between cultural heritage databases. The concomitant obligation for collecting institutions to provide new forms of public access to digital collection content has given further impetus to the pursuit of convergence in both digital and physical contexts.

The link between access to collection information and the attainment of knowledge is most pronounced when considering the literature around digital convergence. Archive and museum informatics specialist Jennifer Trant has noted that the utopian idea of developing seamlessly interconnected digital heritage resources is propelled by the notion of opening up new knowledge horizons to users. She writes, 'Drawing on the desire that all information be available to anyone, anywhere, the vision of an integrated cultural web is portrayed as a powerhouse, latent with the potential of unrealized knowledge' (Trant 2009, 369). The implication is that web technologies will facilitate the release of vast reserves of previously untapped knowledge around collections. Increasingly, siloed professional practices, disciplinary distinctions and time-consuming processes that characterise 'physical' collecting institutions seem at odds with the fluidity, user-centredness and exponentially increasing sophistication of digital technology.

Much of the conversation around convergence presupposes that users' appetite for efficient cross-domain access to online collection databases and other kinds of content has increased at the same rate as technological capacity to deliver these resources. Discussions at a 2009 meeting of CILIP (Chartered Institute of Library and Information Professionals) titled 'Beyond the Silos of the LAMs: Unlocking the benefits of collaboration between libraries, archives and museums' and supported by the UK Society of Archivists, Museums Association and MLA[1] centred on the premise that users 'increasingly expect access to dispersed materials from within a single search environment' (CILIP 2009). As early as 2000, in a report for the European Commission's Information Society Directorate, Lorcan Dempsey emphasised that libraries, archives and museums were striving to emancipate their cultural heritage content via the new potential of digital networks, in recognition of 'their users' desire to refer to intellectual and cultural materials flexibly and transparently, without concern for institutional or national boundaries' (Dempsey 2000, 3). In other words, the primary impediments to what could be termed the 'free flow of knowledge' from resources held by collecting organisations reside in the limitations posed by physical dispersion, for which technological advancements provide an obvious solution.

Such arguments present digital technologies as a panacea for the relative inefficiency of physical collection repositories in disseminating cultural knowledge, and as such, disciplinary distinctions between collecting domains appear obsolete. Furthermore, the restructuring of brick-and-mortar collecting institutions to emulate cross-disciplinary, cross-domain access to collection resources – and 'knowledge' – in the virtual world seems a natural extension of these developments.

Introducing an epistemological perspective

The seductive appeal of digital convergence as a pathway towards universal access to cultural 'knowledge' is, I suggest, founded on the assumption that all kinds of objects in cultural collections (books, documents, images, artefacts, etc.) are equal in their potential to be interpreted for meaning. The examples I have cited imply a presumed equivalence across the 'knowledge' content supplied by the various repositories, and correspondingly, there is no questioning of the ability of users to traverse these knowledge resources seamlessly once digital technology dismantles archaic barriers to access. From this perspective, the information surrounding various collection items – though crafted by the respective repositories – is nevertheless regarded as structurally and epistemologically compatible across institutional boundaries. Like 'objective' scientific facts within a positivist paradigm, individual collection components (objects, digitised documents, photographs, imagery, object records, catalogue entries, exhibition texts, etc.) retain their full information potential despite their de-contextualisation from the body of a specific collection. They can be separated, exchanged and recombined based on the needs of the user and regardless of their original institutional source or provenance, creating the so-called 'Knowledge Commons' that aligns the content of libraries, archives and museums (Curry 2010b). Moreover, we are led to believe, access to information equals access to knowledge, and enabling one will automatically result in possession of the other.

This point of view, perhaps influenced by information science (which has traditionally privileged resource discovery and dissemination over interpretation of content),[2] has given rise to initiatives focussed on producing consistent collection descriptions across sectors in the pursuit of seamless interoperability (see, for example, Johnston and Robinson 2001). New emphasis has been placed on creating generic cross-domain cataloguing tools and standardised vocabularies capable of 'harmonizing cultural metadata,' such as those described by Coburn et al. in their article outlining the development of shared cataloguing protocols for the museum and library communities (Coburn et al. 2010).

However, while the convergence of collecting institutions promises unprecedented access to abundant 'knowledge' reserves, there is a conspicuous absence of discussion about exactly how libraries, archives and museums function as information or knowledge repositories. Precisely what kinds of 'knowledge' are produced by them? Does convergence of cultural collections, either in digital or physical form, necessarily result in greater acquisition of knowledge by users? And what does this discussion indicate about prevalent understandings of the significance of museums, libraries and archives in shaping knowledge around cultural collections? In order to address these questions, it is first necessary to establish a clear understanding of the definition of 'information' in comparison to 'knowledge,' to articulate the relationship between the two concepts, and then to consider how these distinctions apply in relation to cultural collections.

Differentiating data, information and knowledge

The essential differences between 'data,' 'information' and 'knowledge' have long been the subject of epistemological inquiry, as well as forming important themes within other fields, such as the social sciences and information science. And yet distinctions between these concepts seem not to have penetrated discussions in the academic and professional library, archive and museum sectors with regard to the idea of GLAM convergence and hybridisation. Their loose and interchangeable use points to a superficial understanding of what these terms signify. By considering recent scholarship about the nature and creation of knowledge across various disciplinary fields, it is possible to extend theories of knowledge to the idea of convergence and outline a model of knowledge creation against which the benefits of the trend can be evaluated. Ultimately, these concepts become the criteria for assessing the significance of the case study findings presented in this book, enabling evaluation of the extent to which hybridised collecting institutions successfully facilitate knowledge creation and meaningful engagement with museum collections.

A seminal contribution to understanding the differences between information and knowledge was provided in 1991 by Michael K. Buckland, a scholar of library and information science, in his influential article titled 'Information as Thing.' Buckland examined ambiguities around common understandings of the term 'information,' identifying conceptual distinctions between the process of becoming informed, information itself and knowledge, systematically demonstrating that 'information' always takes tangible and physical forms – hence the title of the paper.[3] Buckland emphasises that information is not the same as knowledge, which is only created when human beings encounter and interact with (passive) information and change what they believe or understand as a result (Buckland 1991, 353). The presence of information on its own is no guarantee that knowledge will be produced.

In an article published in 2009 in the *International Social Science Journal* concerning the global distribution and dissemination of knowledge, authors Stehr and Ufer argue a similar point, proposing that the development of digital technologies has indeed allowed for the spread of *information* around the globe at an unprecedented rate, but that global *knowledge* 'remains a highly hypothetical aim' (Stehr and Ufer 2009, 7). Likewise, in a paper presented at the Museums and the Web conference in 2004 titled 'Searching for Meaning: Not Just Records,' Darren Peacock of the National Museum of Australia, together with software developers Derek Ellis and John Doolan, made an important distinction between the superficial availability of online digital collection records and the more complex notion of making these resources meaningful as knowledge to the end user (Peacock, Ellis and Doolan 2004, 1–3). According to these perspectives, the advent of converged collections, where large amounts of collection information from multiple repositories become jointly accessible, cannot on its own guarantee an automatic increase in knowledge about those collections.

The fields of information science (IS) and personal information management (PIM), though normally associated with discussion of information technologies, also intersect usefully with epistemological discussions about the differentiation of data, information and knowledge in library, archive and museum contexts. In a 2010 article intended for a PIM audience, information scientist William Jones offers interesting ideas about how differing approaches to the collection and recording of information might lead to a variety of knowledge outcomes from the same initial data sources. Like Buckland, Jones (2010, 2) identifies information as a 'thing' (as opposed to knowledge, which has no tangible characteristics) and concurs with Stehr and Ufer in proposing that there is interdependency, but not equivalence, between data, information and knowledge. Of particular interest is Jones's discussion of information as the synthesis of data received via cognitive perception, where information comes into being as a tangible record of a perceptual event. In this form, information can be made physically available, manipulated, stored and exchanged in various ways.[4] Notably, information is not the same as 'raw' facts because its content is always already shaped by the subjective processes of perception. In the case of libraries, archives and museums, it follows that collection information must always bear the unique imprint of the authoring institution, being inescapably shaped by the processes and lenses of 'perception' that characterise the documentation practices of each organisation. At this point in the construction of information, the subjective role of individual collecting institutions in embedding particular concepts of significance within the documentation created around collections comes to the fore.

So, if information is tangibly recorded perception of data, what is knowledge? Stehr and Ufer define knowledge as 'a capacity for action. . . . Knowledge enables an actor . . . to set something in motion and to structure reality. Knowledge is thus knowledge about processes' (Stehr and Ufer 2009, 8–9). In other words, having knowledge is not just about the passive consumption of information (i.e. the fact that information is available cannot be equated with access to knowledge). Rather, knowledge results from the ability to make available information personally relevant and useful. Jones takes a similar view, arguing that knowledge comes about through an individual's internalisation of information into the complex world of personal meaning. In this sense, knowledge is fugitive; it exists as an individual's perpetually fluctuating response to the reception of information (Jones 2010, 2). Knowledge is always personal and internalised; it cannot be frozen, recorded and passed on in the same physical ways as information. Knowledge, then, is created when an individual encounters information and uses it to alter his or her reality in some meaningful way.

Donald Hislop, writing on knowledge management and sharing for the *Journal of Information Technology* (2002), has persuasively argued against the idea that knowledge can be effectively transmitted via digital technologies, pointing out that knowledge cannot be reduced to one-way messages transferred via digital networks from a source to a recipient. Hislop builds his critique of the role of information technology in so-called 'knowledge

Same same but different 31

management' by examining philosophies related to the fundamental character of knowledge. He argues that the optimism surrounding information technology as a tool in 'knowledge-sharing' is based on a positivist epistemology that artificially separates knowledge into two discrete components.[5] That is, 'explicit' knowledge, which can be tangibly recorded and therefore transferred from one person to another; and 'tacit' knowledge, which exists within the individual but cannot be expressed verbally, incorporating 'both physical skills and cognitive frameworks' that are embodied and culturally framed (Hislop 2002, 166–67).[6] Because this bipartite view assumes that there is no subjective interference in the communication of 'explicit' knowledge, digital technologies become an ideal conduit for the unimpeded flow of this knowledge between senders and recipients. Precisely this idea underpins Lorcan Dempsey's reference to the 'knowledge networks' (2000, 2) formed through the digital convergence of libraries, archives and museums.

What emerges from the characterisation of information as 'thing' and, conversely, of knowledge as bound to individual context and practice, is that 'knowledge' cannot be transmitted by, or between, repositories (such as libraries, archives and museums), either in physical or digital form. If we accept this approach, it follows that libraries, archives and museums should not be understood as repositories of knowledge at all, but rather of information only – or, as Buckland has written, as a 'species of information retrieval system' (Buckland 1991, 359).

What are the implications of this conceptual approach for convergence of collecting institutions? First of all, the idea that it is only possible to transmit information, rather than knowledge, between collection repositories means that digital convergence of collection records cannot, on its own, achieve a universal diffusion of cultural knowledge on the basis of simply facilitating more streamlined access to collection resources. Likewise, differentiating between information and knowledge negates the ideal of the 'one stop shop' model of physical convergence, complicating the notion that hybrid institutions can automatically deliver knowledge to their end users. Instead, the rationale for convergence needs to do more than simply invoke promises of knowledge gain and articulate the actual strategies, collaborations and processes that will promote meaningful engagements with collections among staff and users. In order to genuinely function as knowledge institutions, the emphasis of GLAM convergence needs to shift from simple integration of collection resources to providing a suitable environment for users to interact with and internalise available collection information. In order to justify convergence on these grounds, user engagements with collection information need to be at least comparable with, or exceed, the possibilities already provided by distinct libraries, archives or museums.

Museum information frameworks

Over time, each collecting domain has developed its own language for describing collections and techniques for collection management, preservation and presentation that create diverse potentials for interacting with information. Museums provide a useful case study for demonstrating how the practices of one type of collecting institution embody various 'ways of seeing' collections – their cultural significance and their utility to the end user – that, in turn, shape the content and structure of collection information and therefore the kinds of knowledge produced around it. This section takes a more detailed look at the ways in which museums function to contextualise their collections, not because these methodologies offer a superior model to that of libraries or archives but, rather, to illustrate the complexities involved in interpreting the content of collections from the standpoint of just a single domain of practice. Because analogous considerations exist for the contextualising processes and physical settings provided by libraries and archives – each producing their own frameworks for understanding content – it becomes possible to glimpse the constellation of engagements possible with collections by encountering them through the 'lens' of various institutional settings. The same considerations complicate the notion that streamlining (or indeed obsolescence) of some of these environments through convergence could lead to improved knowledge outcomes.

Museums are not a homogeneous category but, rather, a conglomeration and crucible of diverse fields of material culture study (even at the level of individual institutions). The intersection of – and often competition between – these fields (including art history, archaeology, social history, natural sciences, etc.) has given rise to numerous attempts to describe the ways in which knowledge is derived through objects. Unsurprisingly, the question of how museums generate meaning around collections has been a motivating and formative concern of museum studies since the 1980s. Inspired by a range of philosophical positions, including positivism, functionalism, phenomenology, post-modernism and affect theory (to name just a few), these critiques have contributed to the dynamic reflexivity of contemporary museology and professional museum practice.

Every museum engages with objects in its own unique way, enacting processes for acquisition, collection documentation, research and communication that are replete with both implicit and explicit judgements about the informational value of each item. Museum theorist Susan Pearce has explored the interconnectedness of objects within museum collections and the impact of various interpretive traditions on understanding the significance of objects. Using the metaphor of an iceberg, Pearce argues that the meanings of collection items should be seen holistically as comprising both the 'tip of the iceberg' – the hard, measurable, quantifiable properties of the individual object that are available to empirical analysis – and the less measurable, amorphous 'below the surface' relationships between the item and the overall collection in which it is embedded, that collection's history, its internal logic and even its physical location (Pearce 1999, 18–19). Similarly, museum scholar Eileen Hooper-Greenhill indicates that the meaning of artefacts in museum contexts is always an interaction between the materiality of the object, its individual associations and the interpretive framework applied to the object in the context of its place in a larger collection that has been assembled according to a particular rationale (Hooper-Greenhill 2000, 103–4). For Hooper-Greenhill and Pearce, a museum object's tangible characteristics, as well as the internal logic of the wider collection, contribute to its knowledge potential.

That the meanings developed around collections are not objective or fixed, but rather 'situated and contextual' (Macdonald 2006, 2), becomes clear when one considers the plethora of methodologies that exist for interpreting museum artefacts. Erwin Panofsky's systematic approach to decoding the symbolic content of artworks, first published in 1939 in his *Studies in Iconology* (see Chapter 1, Panofsky 1970), is an early example of a method for interpreting the meaning of artefacts within the art historical tradition. Some decades later, Thomas Schlereth (1982) and Susan Pearce (1994) produced edited anthologies detailing numerous models for the study of museum objects, each offering different philosophical, disciplinary and practical approaches for interpreting the meaning of collection items. More recently, in their publication of *Significance 2.0* – a methodology for interpreting the cultural values of collections that is used widely in the Australian sector – authors Roslyn Russell and Kylie Winkworth have emphasised that Australian collections owe their diversity to the heterogeneity of the nation's collecting institutions, each with its own history, policies and priorities that have shaped the meanings of items in their care (2009, 2).

One of the most basic steps that museums (and indeed libraries and archives) perform in order to create information around collections is the process of naming objects, or classification. Yet even this apparently straightforward act establishes parameters for interpreting the meaning of a collection item and is deeply influenced by the institution in which the collection is housed. For example, museologist Eileen Hooper-Greenhill has identified the potential for a silver teaspoon to be classified as 'Industrial Art' in the Birmingham City Museum, 'Decorative Art' at Stoke-on-Trent, 'Silver' at the Victoria and Albert Museum and 'Industry' at Kelham Island Museum in Sheffield (1992, 7). Likewise, Sheldon Annis (1994) has highlighted the symbolic nature of museum objects in reference to the thematic relationships that are built between collection objects and the use of artefacts in exhibitions. He notes that, like any symbol, objects in the museum context have no singular, fixed meaning and retain a capacity to be understood in a multitude of ways. He describes them as 'multivocal' and 'polyvalent' – that is, they generate a range of meanings and values (Annis 1994, 21).

The variety of potential outcomes in processes of identification highlights the multiple perspectives from which objects can be understood and associated with one another. This idea is illustrated well by literary theorist Maria Esther Maciel in an article interrogating the idea of the 'unclassifiable' object (Maciel 2006). Here she defines as unclassifiable not only any concept or thing that exists outside of language, but also any object that can be arranged into several taxonomic groupings simultaneously while not being fully contained by any single one. The capacity of objects to move between various typologies highlights the perceived values of objects as contingent upon the classification schemes of the institutions in which they are housed, opening up the possibility for multiple readings of their meaning.

The polysemy of objects is particularly poignant in the context of convergence, as the museum domain has traditionally eschewed universal naming standards (one of the difficulties in identifying common holdings across institutions). The diversity in museum naming conventions highlights the fact that the meaning (and therefore 'knowledge') of objects is not fixed within their physical fabric but, rather, attributed to them through their position in a particular institutional context. Taken together, the diversity between standards of nomenclature across libraries, archives and museums, but also individual organisations within these broad institutional divisions, provides just one example of how a rich, multidimensional information environment for knowledge creation can be produced via the existence of diverse collecting institutions and disciplinary approaches.

The particular techniques that museums employ for contextualising objects, including processes for accessioning, cataloguing, collection management and representation, have been recognised by a number of museology scholars as a distinct epistemological genre (Findlen 2004; Paris 2006). In an article exploring the concept of collecting, Couze Venn identifies museums (though he could just as easily be referring to libraries or archives) not simply as repositories of significant objects but also as cultural artefacts in themselves. According to Venn, collections bear the imprint of the governing epistemologies of the period during which they were assembled and therefore embody the potential to be understood as documents of prevailing culture and intellectual discourse over a particular historical period. Borrowing the words of the phenomenologist philosopher Martin Heidegger, Venn writes that collections bring to light the ways in which societies have approached 'the ordering of the orderable' (Venn 2006, 36), as contained in their chosen classification systems and other forms of schematic grouping, revealing the prevalence of particular world views. Both the conceptual and physical fabrics of a collection are significant in 'enabl[ing] one to interrogate the collection from the point of view of the metacategories operating to constitute the modern architecture of knowledge' (Venn 2006, 37).

In other words, museum interpretive practices represent particular ways of understanding the world – a category for knowing. The work of scholars such as Pearce, Hooper-Greenhill and Venn suggests that the perceived meaning of museum objects can be attributed as much to the physical nature and provenance of the individual item as to the narrative relationships developed between objects within a collection, including the motives (implicit as well as explicit) of the collecting institution that has assembled them. In turn, the reification of these relationships through collection documentation and presentation can influence the kinds of interactions that users experience with objects and the meanings they attribute to them.

Archive and library information frameworks

A brief comparison of the various approaches to the selection and organisation of information employed by archives and libraries provides additional insights into the potential consequences of convergence in bringing together different contexts for knowledge creation.

Just as museum practices of acquisition, collection management, curation and representation give rise to particular kinds of information (as well as providing a tangible illustration of how large quantities of disparate information sources can be organised and associated with one another), libraries and archives represent alternative, equally complex systems for shaping information. In the context of archives, Canadian theorist Terry Cook (2009) has persuasively argued against the idea that archives are passive, neutral repositories of information. He points to archival arrangement and description techniques, along with collection management and even simple administrative activities such as the implementation of destruction schedules and the prioritisation of conservation resources, as active historiographic processes that play an important role in determining the narratives that are eventually produced by historians and others who consult archival materials. Likewise, Elizabeth Yakel has highlighted the subjective, socially constructed nature of archival arrangement practices, noting that archivists often structure archives to reflect an ideal intellectual arrangement, rather than simply describing the actual order of records in their original context (Yakel 2007, 1–2, 10). She argues that the organising principles employed by archivists are not only culturally formed, reflecting and supporting prevalent epistemological frameworks, but also create a feedback loop by establishing parameters for future thought and historical analysis (Yakel 2003, 6). Hence, access and interpretation of original records in archives is pre-determined by the ways in which they are combined and stored with other documents, as well as through the indexes and other finding aids that provide pathways into the material. As museums do with objects, archival methods privilege certain encounters with records and can influence the ways in which their significance is understood.

Libraries can also be seen to promote particular understandings of collections via the selection of content as well as the controlled vocabularies used to classify individual items into thematic groups. In her influential paper titled 'The Power to Name: Representation in Library Catalogues,' Hope Olson (2001) has provided a rigorous analysis of the biases inherent in controlled vocabulary[7] systems such as the widely adopted Library of Congress Subject Headings (LCSH) and Dewey Decimal Classification (DDC). Such systems provide a limited scope for the interpretation of library holdings and force users to conform to rigid hierarchical terminologies in order to access collections.[8] Olson argues that the quest for a universal (homogeneous) descriptive language for naming information in library collections, which is seen as critical in enabling efficient search and retrieval (especially across different collections or institutions), comes at the expense of exploring diverse thematic associations and plural interpretive possibilities of the materials in the collection.[9]

By contrasting the information processing strategies of archives and libraries with those of museums, it is possible to envisage not just museums but all three domains as distinct 'epistemological genres.' Each type of collecting institution (not to mention the variety of approaches that exist at the level of individual organisations) plays an influential formative role on how collection items and the wider groupings into which they are organised are interpreted, named, described and associated with one another, offering a rich tableau of information resources and interactions available to end users. The multiple pathways into collections available via the diversity across, and within, domains create the interface for a constellation of encounters between users and collection objects, giving rise to a multitude of possible 'knowledge' outcomes. Hence, while museums, libraries and archives perhaps function as 'knowledge institutions' in the most generic sense, a more thorough exploration of the diverse contexts for information and knowledge creation across the collecting domains does more to complicate the ideal of seamless convergence on the basis of knowledge compatibility than it does to support it.

Interpretive sustainability: reframing convergence around collection information and knowledge potential

This chapter has examined important conceptual differences between information and knowledge, as well as considering how the collection practices that characterise museums, archives and libraries influence the kind of information generated around collection objects. Understanding that the availability of information – either in the digital realm or in a physically integrated environment – does not automatically translate to the acquisition of knowledge unsettles the basic premise upon which many arguments in favour of convergence rest. As authors Stehr and Ufer conclude in their discussion about knowledge, it is possible that 'one individual has more information than another. It is much more difficult to conclude that one individual commands more knowledge than another' (Stehr and Ufer 2009, 9). So, too, it may be inferred that while a converged collecting institution, either as a digital or physical entity, may contain a larger quantity of tangible information than a discrete library, archive or museum, it cannot be assumed that users will automatically come away with more, or better, knowledge. These considerations form a compelling argument for a shift in focus for converged institutions – one that does not take the production of knowledge as an automatic by-product of institutional integration. In other words, an alternative vision for convergence and hybridisation of collections is needed – one that recognises the importance of the structure and quality of collection information, the specialist work that shapes and contextualises information resources in relation to one another and the opportunities provided for users to make sense of the information.

By considering museums, archives and libraries as individual epistemological genres, it becomes clear that these organisations are differentiated by more than just the physical, typological distinctions across their collection holdings. Each domain represents a distinct framework for the creation of knowledge, employing specific methodologies for interpreting collections and producing information that reflects subjective readings of the identity, value and meaning of objects. The variety of engagements with information that heterogeneous collecting institutions make possible for users represents a valuable and rich interface for cultural interaction and the production of knowledge.

In recognising that museums, libraries and archives offer different but equally subjective and domain-specific approaches to the arrangement and presentation of information, several questions about the assumed benefits of convergence become apparent. For example, to what extent does the value of collecting institutions lie not only in the individual objects and associated records they house, but also in the ways in which these collection items have been organised in relation to one another to reflect an institution's particular epistemological framework?

Considering the way in which information is created and transmitted, we see that libraries, archives and museums cannot automatically be regarded as 'knowledge institutions' or described in similar terms, alluding to their 'knowledge' content. They do not and cannot transmit knowledge. Rather, they offer particular opportunities and settings where users can encounter different forms of *information*, creating knowledge and personal meaning for themselves. By inference, any mechanical co-location or integration of collection resources from different domains, either in a digitally or physically 'converged' environment, will not automatically yield greater knowledge acquisition for end users. However, precisely the opposite result – a reduction in knowledge potential – is a legitimate concern. If the diversity of information ecologies represented by different collecting domains and individual institutions is diminished, is there not also a risk that knowledge creation around collections might likewise contract?

In recognising that the domain-specific and organisational context of objects and information is integral to their potential as sources for 'knowledge,' the challenge in converging museums, libraries and archives becomes the preservation or enhancement of that context, highlighting the polysemous quality of collection objects and offering a diverse menu of information choices to the end user. The complex ways in which information experiences are constructed across the collecting domains suggests there is an advantage in having a large number of diverse institutions – irrespective of whether they are libraries, archives or museums – that can each provide unique engagements with information for the creation of knowledge. From this perspective, fostering an organic, heterogeneous array of collecting institutions – rather than hybrid 'mega-repositories' – could be vital to maintaining the richness and diversity of cultural knowledge. However, based on current understandings evidenced in the use of language surrounding how convergence might advance 'knowledge,' it is not clear whether prevalent approaches to integration take full account of these complexities. Little consideration has been given to how domain-based practices for ordering and making sense of collections operate on the ground in relation to one another. Is their rich informational diversity acknowledged, and can it be effectively nurtured within the scope of converged collection environments – from cultural policy decisions down to collection practices at the level of individual institutions?

If the planning, construction and organisational structure of converged institutions develops in the absence of a strong conceptual rationale and clear strategies for realising the knowledge potential of collections, the risk is that collections will simply continue to function within pre-established modes of operation without drawing any benefit from the model. Of greater concern, though, is that a lack of strategic vision may lead to the implementation of staffing structures and administrative processes that actually interfere with an organisation's ability to offer their users meaningful engagements with collections. The idea of 'interpretive sustainability,' then, can be considered

Same same but different 39

central to any consideration of how the collecting domains can be successfully integrated and hybridised.

The ways in which converged organisations can effectively create the conditions necessary for users to make meaning around the collections – acknowledging and leveraging existing disciplinary approaches to the arrangement of collection information and the interpretation of collection objects – have not (until now) been questioned. The case study findings presented in the following two chapters represent the first such examination of the impact of convergence on interpretive museum practices.

Notes

1 The British Museums, Libraries and Archives Council, launched in 2000 by the UK government to provide joint strategic direction, promote standards and allocate funding across the collecting domains, as well as providing policy advice to government. It was active until 2010, when funding was discontinued.
2 See Hjorland's outline of the conceptual basis of information science and, in his view, its flawed grounding in nineteenth century positivism (Hjorland 2000).
3 Buckland views every kind of object as potentially informative. Under this broad definition, museum artefacts, written documents, audio-visual materials, images and even natural found objects all have information status (Buckland 1991, 353–55).
4 See also Hjorland's citation of the American Association of Information Science (ASIS) definition of information, which is similar (Hjorland 2000, 32).
5 Hjorland (2000, 32–33) also highlights that the proposition that interconnection of digital data files equates to the true interconnection of ideas is based on a nineteenth century positivism, which does not acknowledge the contingency of information to its source. Hence, the information produced by libraries, archives and museums carries its own institutional legacy and cannot necessarily be transposed into a converged collection context without either obscuring authorship or losing informational identity. Such considerations in turn raise questions about the ability to streamline information from diverse sources – or indeed the possibility of a true flow of 'knowledge' – in a converged collection environment.
6 The notion of 'explicit' knowledge can be paralleled with the definition of 'information,' as described by Jones and Buckland. Correspondingly, 'tacit' knowledge bears a resemblance to Jones's concept of knowledge as personally embodied and embedded. Jones avoids compartmentalising knowledge into two types, understanding 'information' as a prerequisite (and phase) in the development of knowledge but not encapsulating it in a particular and finite form.
7 Also termed 'bibliographic control.'
8 In recognising the inflexibility of library naming systems, Sarah Anne Murphy (2005) has written about the vital role of the reference librarian in collaborating with users to facilitate successful retrieval of relevant reference materials. She identifies searching a reference collection as a narrative hermeneutic process, where the user and the librarian work together to re-interpret and re-frame the reference query until it becomes compatible with the allowable search limits, or language, of the library catalogue. Also crucial to Murphy's argument is the significance of the personal interaction between the reference librarian and

the user – an aspect of the library experience that seems largely omitted in the context of online access to library catalogues.
9 Historian David McKitterick (2006) approaches a similar point in his account of the development of library collections in England and continental Europe in the sixteenth century. His description of the slow and un-systematic crystallisation of formalised principles for the organisation of library collections, not to mention the gradual development of librarianship as a profession, demonstrates that there is no intrinsic 'natural' order according to which books can be classified and, therefore, assigned meaning.

3 Process conflict

Interpreting museum collections within the convergence context

> *You know, you would never have a standalone museum where collections weren't considered to be an important thing, whereas I think they have been really strongly sidelined here.*
>
> —heritage collections team member, Maunga Tapu

In the previous two chapters, I have argued that GLAMs are characterised by particularities in the content and organisation of collection information. These differences establish and reproduce parameters around the kinds of interpretive engagements that users (professional staff as well as public stakeholders) can have with collections. Rather than revealing a fundamentally aligned (and therefore reconcilable) set of collection practices, this analysis instead exposes the collections sector as a heterogeneous conglomeration of information environments that contextualise the meanings and values of collection materials in a multitude of domain- and institution-specific ways. According to this analysis, the conflation of GLAMs as 'knowledge institutions' as justification for convergence obscures important distinctions between the domains at the level of meaning-making. If knowledge about anything (including collections) is produced only by individuals engaging with available configurations of information in the context of their own personal needs, intentions and existing understanding, then differences in the ways in which collection information is structured have a profound influence on the kinds of collection 'knowledge' that can be produced. Equating information with knowledge – as evidenced in the rhetoric around 'knowledge institutions' – ignores the influence of information frameworks on the production of meaning around collections. The risk of this elision is that the individual collection practices of museums, libraries and archives, which represent a multidimensional array of potential information encounters, will be overlooked as newly hybridised collecting institutions come to fruition. Paradoxically, this convergence scenario therefore has the potential to reduce opportunities for knowledge creation. Converged GLAMs risk being reduced to bureaucratic amalgamations, prioritising and perhaps achieving administrative efficiency but doing so at the expense of the vibrant potentials for the thought-provoking, multivalent encounters with collection materials that the interaction between different information frameworks could ideally produce. Is this concern justified?

Prior to the research outlined in this book, it has been difficult to offer a response to this question. The limited existing research is at stark odds with the prevalence of cross-domain collaboration and convergence occurring worldwide. Much of the literature supports the notion of convergence as a worthy ideal, but authors of the few published international studies dealing with collaboration and integration of libraries, museums and archives acknowledge that existing research is at best fragmentary, with few surveys examining the breadth, implications and success of such projects.[1] Very few examples of full institutional (or 'physical') convergence have been examined in comparison to studies of isolated, project-specific collaboration between independent organisations or cases confined to digital convergence.

Having established a rationale for 'interpretive sustainability' in theory, there is a clear opportunity to investigate the effects of convergence on museum processes of meaning-making. As I have outlined earlier, it is beyond the scope of this book to undertake an equally granular interrogation of convergence from the perspectives of each of the collecting domains. However, because museums are fundamentally and self-consciously engaged in interpretation of collections to a greater extent than either libraries or archives (see Chapter 2, 32–35), they are, arguably, more vulnerable to the potential negative impacts of convergence on the creation of knowledge and meaning. It is not unreasonable, then, to focus on museum practices in assessing the real-world impact of GLAM integration and hybridisation.

This chapter presents the findings of research conducted at three converged collecting institutions, chosen for their significance within the development of convergence as an approach to restructuring cultural facilities in Australia and New Zealand. While institutional convergence has the potential to involve cultural organisations of all sizes, in Australia and New Zealand, the trend has generally manifested itself at the local government level and in regional areas (Boaden and Clement 2009). Convergence of museums, libraries, archives and galleries is often associated with the concept of cultural 'hubs' or precincts, where various facilities are clustered together in order to provide a focal destination point for the community and tourists, as well as encouraging the sharing of audiences through the proximity of venues. Regional and local government areas have been acutely affected by aging infrastructure and stakeholder demands for better cultural facilities. Convergence offers a solution to rationalising expenditure while simultaneously responding to community expectations. Cultural organisations in outer metropolitan and regional locations are significant for local populations that are geographically remote from major state and national cultural institutions.[2] Converged institutions in these areas offer a fertile and compelling opportunity to examine whether the hybridisation of physical spaces, disciplinary expertise and operational functions supports the creation of dynamic and meaningful engagements with collections.

A brief note on methodology

The three institutions outlined in this book – referred to here by the pseudonyms Lonehill, Westlands and Maunga Tapu to protect the anonymity of the respondents – share important commonalities that qualify them for cross-case comparison.[3] All were established as newly converged entities between 2003 and 2007 through the amalgamation of previously existing and autonomous collecting organisations. They represent experiments in a new kind of organisational and management structure, bringing together collection professionals with a range of disciplinary backgrounds and experience under the expectation of collaboration and cross-fertilisation of skills. The institutions were established to enable more efficient expenditure of ratepayer money for the provision of cultural infrastructure. Significantly, they represent a new kind of repository, where various combinations of works of art, museum and local history collections, library holdings and archival records are housed side by side under the premise of improving their value to users through joint collection access and inventive cross-disciplinary research and public programs.

For each case study, official documents, media reports and advertising materials were consulted to provide background, history and statistical information on each facility.[4] I visited each institution and interviewed staff working across a range of operational areas but united through their involvement in museum interpretive practice, including collection development (how an institution shapes its collections by strategically acquiring and disposing of objects), documentation and description (conducting research into and classifying individual items and collections, establishing thematic connections between collected material) and the development of collection-based public programs (curating permanent and temporary exhibitions, compiling publications, etc.).

Using a questionnaire developed from key themes that emerged during the literature review, extended semi-structured interviews were conducted with 39 staff members in total as well as three representatives of non-government collections sector umbrella bodies that had been involved in supporting converged institutions. I assessed how workers in each organisation understood the effects of convergence on their ability to manage, document, interpret and render access to different kinds of collection materials.

The interview transcripts provided an abundance of primary data from which to analyse the impact of convergence. Having trained and worked in specific disciplinary contexts, the practices of collection professionals in museums, galleries, archives and libraries are fundamental in shaping the ways in which different types of collections are assembled, evaluated, classified, documented and presented to users. At the same time, staff members are also at the frontline of organisational changes that directly impact their daily practices. Through convergence, they were subject to revisions of institutional goals and priorities, the redefinition of role descriptions and new expectations regarding levels of collaboration across collection areas.

For these reasons, the accounts of staff working in converged institutions provide a unique window into the conceptual and structural shifts involved in convergence as well as whether the projected advantages of domain hybridisation materialise in day-to-day practice and service delivery. Much like 'street-level bureaucrats' – a term coined by Michael Lipsky (1980) in his influential research on the discretionary agency of frontline public servants in implementing policy – collection professionals who have firsthand experiences of the convergence process provide otherwise unobtainable information about alterations to specialist practices, workflows, staff communication and management. Combined with information obtained from documentary sources, analysis of their frank accounts of convergence reveals the influence of the model on the interpretive context of collections and, in turn, the perceived meanings and potential for knowledge creation around collection materials.

I now turn to the findings of the case study interviews to explore the impact of convergence on the interpretation of museum collections. The thematic analysis of the interview data focuses on aspects of museum expertise and practice that have direct bearing on the creation of meaning and attribution of value to collections. This includes consideration of so-called 'back-of-house' functions, such as acquisition procedures, collection research and documentation and conservation, as well as the use of collections in the development of 'forward-facing' projects, such as permanent and temporary displays and educational and other public programs. The impact of convergence on the potential for the cultural significance of museum objects to be explored and communicated emerges as a central theme.

Rather than treating each case independently, I have chosen to present the findings as a transversal thematic content analysis so that significant issues can be considered comparatively across all three cases simultaneously. While this is an efficient and accessible way to deal with a large quantity of information, it can create the impression of an artificially neat compartmentalisation of the data, partially obscuring interrelationships and contingencies between various thematic threads running through the research (not to mention the complexities inherent in actual practice). To mitigate this effect and underscore the interconnectedness between themes, I have included as much primary transcript material as possible, with the intention of foregrounding different nuances in the responses of interviewees and acknowledging overlap across thematic boundaries.

Museum interpretive practices in hybrid GLAMs

Although the content, scope and histories of the museum collections at the institutions studied for this research vary, all were initially developed by local historical societies. By the time they were incorporated into their respective organisations, their collections consisted of an array of objects, including social history and technological artefacts, archaeological and indigenous materials, artworks, archival images and photographs. At the time the institutions were established, it would be fair to say that all the museum collections in question were inconsistently (or very poorly) documented and conserved. They existed within very loose policy frameworks, administered by a mixture of paid, qualified staff and volunteers.

Importantly, what these collections had in common was their abundant potential for development, research and contextualisation. They were all under-documented and under-interpreted, sometimes according to even the most basic standards of accessioning (i.e. object classification and naming, recording of provenance, numerical registration into the collection, etc.). Indeed, the accounts of many respondents in this research indicate the degree to which this potential had (or had not) been realised, providing valuable insights into the performance and efficacy of museum practices within the convergence model.

Reconnecting collections

Developing collections through strategic acquisitions (and disposals) and identifying their cultural values through research and documentation represent a first stage in establishing the meanings of cultural material as well as creating the possibility for items held in different repositories to be contextually linked to one another. At Lonehill and Maunga Tapu, the primary benefit of convergence was the amalgamation (or establishment of formal relationships) between museum and local studies collections. Respondents identified local studies as an area of natural crossover between museums and municipal libraries. In this way, convergence indeed provided a mechanism for integrating thematically linked collections of objects, documents and photographs that had previously existed in separate collecting institutions. This 'reunification' was realised through joint databases and thematic linkages as well as enhanced research potential and convenience for visitors and other users.

At Maunga Tapu, the local studies collection had not existed officially prior to the convergence, having been established in the form of a regional research centre through the restructuring process. Serving as a research gateway, the purpose of the local studies section was to provide access to both its own study materials and collections (and staff expertise) across the institution. The former manager of the organisation noted that this local studies facility was perhaps the single area of the institution that actually functioned effectively as an example of full convergence:

> There wasn't really much evidence of an integrated service other than in the ... research centre. And that's where anyone who was seriously interested in the history of [the region] would be able to go to one space, ask their question and be dealt with by a range of experts and have one suite of resources – including collections of artefacts – but also the documentary heritage of [the region]. That made a lot of sense for that kind of enquiry.
>
> (former manager of Maunga Tapu)

Convergence activated the potential for informal thematic connections between local studies collections (commonly located and staffed through libraries) and museums (often originating with local historical societies) to be recognised and legitimised through structural integration. Greater collaboration between library, local studies and museum staff elevated the research capacity of each respective section, enhancing the development of programs and exhibitions and extending research access for public users.

The important relationship between local studies and museum collections was underscored when considering the consequences of the separation of these areas, as occurred at Westlands.

Westlands was established in a regional centre where the library remained separate from the converged institution (which incorporated the local museum, art gallery and a community arts facility). During the restructuring process, the local studies collection was divided from the museum and set up in the library – a move that seems to have been justified on the basis of the typological differences between the items in the local studies versus museum collection. The local studies officer, who had previously been involved with the museum collection, described how this process divorced related objects from one another physically, stating, 'It's like I have the left arm and they have the right arm.' For her, this situation not only resulted in two closely related collections being subject to different access policies and conservation regimes but also limited the narrative links that could have been derived from them through a unified approach:

> There were family 'boxes' with a mix of items, and that was split, which is sad now because over at [Westlands] . . . they don't know that there's all this additional material. . . . They are not aware of the associations.
>
> (local studies officer, city council library service)

Not only was a thematically linked collection physically split but the separation of the local studies officer – with her considerable local knowledge and familiarity with the content of the museum collection – from the remaining museum staff also fractured the ability of employees to collaborate around the interpretation of the collection. Given the seemingly obvious connections between the two collections, the decision to exclude the local studies collection from the planning for Westlands is puzzling, suggesting a fundamental misunderstanding of the conceptual rationale for the project by the local government authority.

Acquisitions and collection development

While the integration of local studies and museum collections clearly appears advantageous for access, research, documentation and interpretation of objects, other aspects of the operating environment brought about through convergence were not perceived as equally beneficial for developing collections or extending understandings of their mutually reinforcing significance.

According to respondents in all three case studies, the main limitation to strategic collection development of museum collections under convergence was the lack of budget allocation for new acquisitions – a symptom of converged funding models that underestimate the ongoing operational costs of integrated institutions.

The visual arts coordinator at Lonehill – a primarily curatorial role – underlined the discrepancy between this area of budgetary shortfall and the size of her organisation, describing how collections staff were compelled to devise various unofficial mechanisms for acquiring new objects to sidestep the lack of funds set aside for this purpose:

> Surprisingly, the [smaller] gallery that I came from had a higher acquisitions budget. The [Lonehill] museum and the art gallery don't actually have a direct acquisitions fund at all. . . . So the way that acquisitions happen is by [the museum and social history coordinator] and I sort of 'creatively' massaging our exhibition budget, or structure a contract where you might get the exhibition for free, frame their work and then get so many prints. It's actually interesting, given our operations budget, that we don't have an acquisitions budget.
>
> (visual arts coordinator, Lonehill)

Members of the heritage collections team at Maunga Tapu expressed frustration about the shortage of funds for acquisitions. Like their counterparts at Lonehill, they, too, 'creatively' manipulated their existing budgets, saving small yearly allocations in order to build up an acquisitions war chest.

At Westlands, a moratorium had been imposed on acquisitions to the museum collection following the convergence restructure. The local council justified the hiatus on the basis of a shortage of additional storage space and the poor documentation of the existing collection. While founded on legitimate concerns, the prohibition on acquisitions nevertheless proved problematic in terms of collection development around important local themes. As the curator pointed out, the organisation had missed opportunities to make purchases (and even accept donations) of potentially significant objects on account of the inflexibility of the rule:

> Certainly, there have been objects come our way that have been offered for the museum to buy, but we haven't been able to buy them . . . I think that there needs to be the opportunity to purchase things if we need to, if they are significant.
>
> (curator, museum and art gallery, Westlands)

Budget decisions not to acquire, made by management staff or local municipal funding authorities, contributed to various degrees of stagnation in the development of the museum collections. At Westlands and Maunga Tapu, such restrictions had been in place for several years. While it could be argued that the lack of sufficient funding for acquisitions is not a problem confined to or necessarily caused by convergence, it would seem that implementation of such restructures as part of a program for achieving financial efficiency produced management decisions that were not in the best interests of museum collection development. Furthermore, as I discuss later, convergence also amplified the discrepancies between relatively small funding allocations to museum collections and the larger budget allowance for library operations.

Collection documentation and description

Following the stages of conventional curatorial and collection management workflow, consideration of collection development policies and acquisition processes brings us to the description and documentation of museum objects (i.e. cataloguing, documentation, research) in converged organisations. For the most part, participants in this research acknowledged the positive outcomes of convergence on collection documentation, although improvements in this area were attributed mainly to the official incorporation of previously volunteer-run historical society or community collections into a formal collecting institution, rather than to the effects of integrating different collecting domains per se.

Starting from what was often a very low base, the implementation of basic standards and procedures for museum cataloguing, performed (sometimes for the first time) by professional staff, was a clear benefit for museum collections brought into converged institution environments. Respondents at Westlands in particular were keen to point out the lack of documentation around their museum collection prior to the convergence restructure. A professionalised institutional structure allowed for specialist curatorial roles to be created, helping to establish an environment where consistent collection documentation procedures could begin to take place.

Professionalisation also resulted in the drafting of policy frameworks for acquisitions and collection management. The collections officer at Westlands claimed that a benefit of her converged role description was the ability to assess and improve the respective standards of collection management and documentation across both the museum and visual arts collections. However, her account mirrored those of most other participants in acknowledging that collection themes and development priorities remained quite separate, and often incompatible, across the different collection areas.

In general, however, a clear and binding articulation of institution-wide collection aims and strategies for collaboration remained elusive. At Lonehill, a consequence of lack of clarity around the rationale for the convergence, a poorly designed organisational structure and a shortage of staff delayed implementation of formal museum policies and procedures, exacerbating the effects of insufficient resources to maintain basic collection management standards. The initial convergence structure did not make provision for any staff to catalogue and research the museum collection.

Furthermore, an employee from an exclusively library background was installed as the manager of the museum collection, leading to the alteration of fundamental museum procedures. The staff member drew on her knowledge of library practice to make unilateral judgements about the appropriateness of museum cataloguing procedures, potentially disrupting the consistency of the museum's existing records:

> The first thing we did was get rid of the accession register – just put it to the side. We figured out a way to do our [object] numbers.... From my point of view, it just felt like it was a very labour-intensive process, whereas we get a book in, catalogue it – I mean 99% of library books are catalogued, whereas with the museum collection, 90% of it wasn't catalogued.
>
> (information and library collections coordinator, Lonehill)

Using library conventions as her only available point of reference, this staff member focussed her attention on improving the 'efficiency' of the museum cataloguing process without considering the possible value of registers as an initial documentary layer in recording the entry of objects into museums before formal accessioning takes place. What this example illustrates is the potential damage caused to collection documentation through inappropriate recruitment of staff to roles requiring specialist disciplinary expertise and experience.

Managing differences between domain-based approaches to collection documentation came to fore in a number of other respondents' accounts of their work in converged settings. In particular, museum staff across the three case studies encountered difficulties in creating institution-wide recognition of the time-intensive nature of museum cataloguing, research and collection documentation (especially when set in sharp relief against the relative efficiency of library processes). In turn, this had a knock-on effect on distribution of resources across the institution. As one of the heritage collection team members at Maunga Tapu explained:

> What we've found is gross discrepancies between what one aspect of the business gets as opposed to the other. I think that heritage [collection] has been very badly impinged upon. The collections, in terms of funding . . . that allows us to do core work: cataloguing, the day-to-day stuff – and that's the bread and butter of a museum's work – but with convergence. . . . You know, you would never have a standalone museum where collections weren't considered to be an important thing, whereas I think they have been really strongly sidelined here. The lack of money allows us to do less and less than would normally be done in a museum business.
>
> (heritage collections team member, Maunga Tapu)

Another member of the same team noted that the separation of collections and exhibition development into different departments within the museum section of the organisation had marginalised the profile of documentation and research of the collection. In combination with the difficulty in communicating museum priorities to an unsympathetic director (who had come from a library background) and the lack of appeal of collection documentation to potential sponsors, the status of essential museum work was further downgraded in a joint collection environment:

> You know, exhibitions is kind of the sexy side of the business, so it's much easier to raise funds for exhibitions, I think, than it is for the stuff that we do. . . . Because it's much easier to, say, sell an exhibition to a firm, or a business. [You can't say,] 'How would you like to sponsor some cataloguing?'
>
> (manager, heritage collections, Maunga Tapu)

This respondent expressed general frustration about lack of resources for labour-intensive but low-profile activities such as registration and accessioning as well as for researching the provenance and historical contexts of individual objects. At the same time, he signalled his ongoing professional commitment to these tasks, highlighting the acute importance of description and documentation in determining the quality of all other subsequent collection programs:

RESPONDENT 1: Because once you understood that ethic you would understand that you are going to get a better exhibition, you are going to get a better public program, better research –
RESPONDENT 2: Better marketing –
RESPONDENT 1: All of those things will start to cascade out of that work that you've got to put in right at the beginning.
RESPONDENT 2: And that's one of those things – I guess you can never expect anybody to know the reality of your job, but it's so hard to explain to people how long cataloguing takes!
(heritage collections team interview, Maunga Tapu)

Likewise, the collections officer at Westlands emphasised the fundamental importance of collection documentation and management in shaping future uses of the museum's holdings:

> I am conscious of the fact that big strategic decisions about the collection can't be made until we're all fully aware of exactly what's there and exactly how it's organised and what we've got and what we don't have. So, I feel as though I'm building the foundation into some kind of order.
>
> (collections officer, museum and art gallery, Westlands)

Crucially, these extracts highlight the long-tail benefit of collection documentation in extending the capacity for users to eventually access and engage with collection objects both physically and intellectually. However, many of the respondents' accounts indicated insufficient recognition of the significance of basic collection work at their institutions.[5] For example, some respondents described the tendency to defer original research and cataloguing of museum collections indefinitely to meet short-term programming deadlines. The collections officer at Westlands noted that this approach favoured use of parts of the collection that were already well-researched and, conversely, discouraged time-intensive investigation of less well-documented objects or research of underdeveloped themes. In these ways, the staffing and resource shortages described by the participants could combine to produce potential detrimental effects in every stage in the life cycle of museum collections and, down the line, the extent and depth to which users can interact with the full scope of collections and the information surrounding them.

Converging collection databases and access

As discussed in Chapter 1 (page 15), the promise of a 'virtual Wunderkammer' via online database integration has been a strong motivating factor driving both digital and physical convergence. As an extension of description and documentation of collections, the potential for increased cross-domain collection database access was discussed by a number of respondents in this research.

At Westlands, the collections officer spoke about reviewing the documentation of the museum and visual arts collections around joint subject keywords to eventually facilitate research across both collections, even though she acknowledged that the pursuit of cross-collection search capability was her own personal initiative, rather than a strategic goal of the organisation. A similar project was underway at Lonehill, where the purchase of new library collection management software would enable keyword searches across the library catalogue, subscribed electronic publications and potentially the museum collection database. These efforts signal some recognition by converged institutions of the potential to create thematic linkages between objects and information held in separate digital databases, with the hope of streamlining and enriching research capacity for collection professionals and collection users alike.

However, other respondents identified a number of impediments to database compatibility and interoperability. One criticism centred around the problem of different terminologies between the collecting domains, leading

Process conflict 53

to difficulties in reconciling naming conventions in joint databases. For example, the heritage collections team at Maunga Tapu noted that the staff member charged with cataloguing archival materials at their institution had to repurpose a museum collection database system to suit archival cataloguing needs, leading to clumsy object descriptions and the inability to clearly account for record series.

Importantly, some participants highlighted broader epistemological consequences in altering domain-based cataloguing and documentation structures. One collections and exhibitions officer from Lonehill explained that the compromises inherent in adapting terminologies and information fields to fit the format of library-based software forced compromises in the conventional description and diversity of information recorded around museum or visual arts collections. He warned that all-encompassing databases were likely to be overly generalist in their nature, forcing out nuanced, specialised information categories in favour of a one-size-fits-all framework:

> It's like when you're designing a car to be either a racing car or a taxi; it's hard to get one that will do both. You're going to have a vehicle in the middle that's not a very good taxi and not a very good racing car.
>
> (collections and exhibitions officer, art gallery, Lonehill)

Elaborating on this further, a former senior staff member of a national collections sector body who was also interviewed as part of this research outlined the essential differences between collections information that shape the documentary practices of the different domains and therefore the record-keeping and documentary approaches employed by them:

> Librarians anchor their information management to some very clear givens. For example, almost everything has a named author, almost everything has a title, almost everything has a date of publication, so they've got some really strong givens, and I can imagine a librarian feeling totally at sea if they didn't have those anchoring points. Whereas the museum world is completely used to things not having [a known] maker, not having an agreed name or multiple names. . . . You often don't know the date or even the century when the object was manufactured, created, or its evolution. So you are dealing with uncertainty, rather than certainty, in the museum world.
>
> And I think archivists are a little in between because they are dealing with unique materials, and they might be authored materials, but the author might have to be deduced, rather than finding it on the title page . . .

So I think the way in which systems have evolved to document those sorts of collections, it's not just driven by the individuals involved in those professions and the way they are trained. It's also that the starting point for one profession is fixed knowledge, and the starting point for the other professions is 'nothing is fixed.'

(former senior staff member, national collections sector agency)

This extract highlights how the ways in which information is organised in collection databases – and the architecture of those databases – frames the information content within certain epistemological contexts, ranging from empirically defined, fixed, positivist attribution of knowledge to more interpretive and contingent understandings of objects. The reconfiguration and renaming of collection information to achieve compatibility across databases represents more than a simple reorganisation of content. Rather, it potentially constitutes a fundamental alteration in the kinds of information and, therefore, knowledge produced around collections.

Notably, however, such considerations appear to be largely academic in reference to the case studies used for this research. Participants from both Lonehill and Maunga Tapu, whose websites offered some degree of database convergence and cross-collection search capability, acknowledged that the provision of access to diverse collections had been underutilised. A member of the exhibitions team at Maunga Tapu described the online search function on his institution's website as 'pedestrian,' with little appeal to public users. Similarly, the library manager at Lonehill acknowledged that her institution had little evidence to suggest that online users were utilising the ability to search subject themes across the organisation's holdings.

It seems that the potential for digital convergence of collection databases – and the promise of interconnected access to thematically linked information sources – has not been realised so far. The task of reconciling different documentary traditions and terminological conventions is cumbersome and time-consuming, unlikely to be completed given the other pressures on staff in converged institutions.

The practical difficulties in implementing genuinely streamlined digital database access across various kinds of collections are indicative of a broader set of concerns around the impact of integrated organisational structures on the behind-the-scenes activities associated with museum collection development, documentation and management. The identification of collection values, achieved through dedicated research of individual objects, forms the bedrock of subsequent interpretive activities, including exhibition development. Community engagement with collections, enabled via exhibitions, programs and other forms of access, generates the public appreciation for collections that justifies ongoing council expenditure on museum staff and collection budgets. Yet without some pre-existing understanding of the significance of a collection, it is difficult to justify the resources required to document and conserve it. In this way, museum collections can become trapped in a circular 'catch-22' scenario: if a collection is chronically under-researched and there is insufficient 'start-up' investment for collection work, the foundations for higher-order interpretation will never be established. Staff may find it difficult to argue for increased funding for poorly documented (and therefore low profile) parts of the collections, objects will simply be warehoused, and the potential to create meaningful connections across and between collecting areas will be diminished.

Although this problem is not restricted to converged collecting institutions, integrated staffing structures and competition between an increased number of operational areas can accentuate the situation. When museum workers compete to sustain their visibility to management against higher profile public-facing parts of an organisation – such as a library service – making the case for resourcing already marginalised museum collections becomes an even greater challenge.

Exhibitions

Permanent, temporary and travelling exhibitions, as well as other interfaces for visitor (or 'user') interactions with collections (such as educational programs, guided tours, publications, online forms of access, etc.), are the end products of cataloguing, documentation and research of museum collections. Exhibitions are fundamentally interpretive, layering higher-order conceptual abstraction over the interpretive content of collection documentation and forging new thematic and narrative connections between objects, histories, places and people. For this reason, a detailed analysis of the case studies in reference to exhibitions and public programs is central to understanding the extent to which GLAM convergence enhances or inhibits museum interpretive processes.

A common feature of the institutions studied for this research was the demarcation of publicly accessible 'museum' spaces into so-called 'permanent' (or 'semi-permanent') and 'temporary' exhibition areas, with small, adjunct displays often also located in common circulation zones, parts of the library or in research areas. Accordingly, this section of the findings focuses on respondents' accounts of the provision of these two types of exhibitions in their organisations, including museum work associated with exhibition planning and development, exhibition design, installation and maintenance.

Permanent exhibitions

Across all the case studies, participants in the research pointed to significant problems associated with thematic content of the permanent exhibitions at their institutions, where displays were expected to communicate significant information about local regions and cultural groups as well as clear chronologies of important events. Respondents were dissatisfied with the representativeness, accuracy and narrative cohesion of permanent exhibitions, which was compounded by a lack of resources to achieve regular rotation of objects and redevelopment of displays.

A common observation among the participants was that the design and content of permanent exhibitions had originally been developed and installed by 'outsiders' – contracted curators and designers – who did not have the necessary pre-existing knowledge of the local area and its people to produce coherent, relevant narratives. For example, the manager at Westlands was critical of the selection of objects used for the permanent display, which he perceived as having failed to identify potent historical, political and cultural discourses that were constitutive of local cultural identities and continued to shape the experiences of people living in this regional, rural area:

> We all recognise that the museum has flaws in its service to the public. It is so object-based, it doesn't tell a cogent narrative. You just come in and turn right. The first thing you see is a small Aboriginal display, which mixes things given by European settlers to Aborigines with stone tools and wooden hunting weapons. Then you go on to a Chinese [object] made from an old biscuit tin, and then you've got some old swimming costumes, and then you have a steam engine. So, I pity the viewer who comes in here to learn about this town – it's hard to put it all together . . .
>
> We want to fix that and have a more cogent narrative while at the same time not coming down on one side or the other. So, talking about the disputes between the original inhabitants, the settlers, and the people on the stock route, which meant that there were gunshots fired. That story needs to be told; not this person was right or this person was wrong. We need to show this conflict is still here now – this conflict is still going on about who has land and who has assets and what you can do with it. That's what we want to do. And talk about agriculture, mining, farming from both sides, industry, the various failed housing developments that went through here, crime and punishment, really give people a sense of, well, that was [this town], but this is also really typical of a country town, this is how they developed.
>
> (manager of Westlands)

Process conflict 57

As the passage demonstrates, this participant identified the permanent exhibition as having abundant but unrealised potential in promoting active and constructive engagement with issues of local importance among the population of the town and surrounding region. Instead, the narrative presented within the displays is disjointed and ad hoc, providing only glimpses of significant cultural groups, industries, events and social changes, without exploring thematic connections between these individual parts or the relationships between local narratives and those of other rural communities.

While these deficiencies cannot be laid solely at the feet of convergence, the situation suggests that the conceptual rational for the physical integration of collecting areas – in supposedly expanding opportunities for meaningful engagement with collections – was not at the forefront in the planning phases of the project. Senior staff at both Lonehill and Maunga Tapu likewise observed that permanent displays at their institutions had been developed hurriedly, with abbreviated exhibition development deadlines that prevented, for example, curatorial consultation with communities about significant local themes:

> And what happened with the [organisation] was that that semi-permanent exhibition went up very, very quickly, without too much thought, I think, and it's not cohesive. So [the museum and social history coordinator] and I are organising for a facilitator to come in and for us to develop a group of people, including the historical society and interested people from the community, to talk about what could be there.
> (team leader, art gallery and collections, Lonehill)

> The way that the building was developed, what's on display was actually a bit of a rush job.
> (project and technical administrator, exhibitions, Maunga Tapu)

It was not possible for curatorial development to take full account of what objects were available for use in the exhibitions, their relative significance to one another, nor their representativeness in regard to the history and people of the area. Instead, exhibitions were established on the basis of partial knowledge of collections and their context. Where external consultants were employed, whatever expertise was gained during the exhibition development process was subsequently lost once they had completed their contracts and departed. In the prevailing context of funding shortages for museum activities within converged institutions (see Chapter 1), the fixed design of the exhibition spaces and hardware at all the case study institutions meant that initial shortcomings in permanent displays turned into ongoing legacies, as museum staff could not make structural changes to the exhibitions without incurring large capital costs. The exhibitions therefore remained static and largely unreflective of discoveries made in the course of ongoing collections research, nor could they accommodate themes emerging from modified school curricula or shifting ideas about the heritage of the local population:

> What we're tackling at the moment are funding issues to do with how we go about refreshing those [permanent] galleries. One way we're going to disenfranchise our public is to be seen to not really care much and not investing energy into keeping the place vibrant.
>
> (manager, exhibitions, Maunga Tapu)

In other words, unchanging, poorly funded permanent exhibitions have the potential to threaten the sustainability of institutions by implicitly communicating a disregard for the value of local heritage and culture to local users and visitors alike. With exhibition areas functioning as the primary interface between museums and a large proportion of their audiences, any institution that neglects the development and maintenance of its displays – especially a converged organisation whose operation is paid for by council rates – risks alienating the community of stakeholders that fund its ongoing operations.

Temporary exhibitions

In contrast to relatively stagnant permanent displays, temporary exhibitions were a focal point of all the case studies involved in this research. Most institutions had a very active program of changing exhibitions.

In this regard, one benefit of convergence, often cited by participants across all the cases, was greater access and flexibility in the use of exhibition spaces, especially when new facilities were constructed to house integrated institutions. The capacity to spread larger exhibitions across multiple zones (i.e. library, research centre or general circulation spaces) not only increased the potential to accommodate a wider variety of travelling and in-house exhibitions but also had the additional advantage of promoting the growth of new audience groups across collecting areas:

> I'd say one of the benefits of convergence is that we can co-locate exhibitions like Great Collections. . . . And certainly, it introduces new audiences in particular to the gallery. So you get people that don't normally go there – who might go to the library, borrow a book, wander through the museum but not often go to the gallery. But if they see that 'oh, there's a motorbike over there at the gallery' . . . It's a different type of clientele, so I think it does help with audience development.
>
> (museum and social history coordinator, Lonehill)

Process conflict 59

Convergence resulted in multipurpose collection spaces, creating capacity for a more diverse range of exhibitions and inviting broader access by a likewise variegated audience.

However, the prevalence of touring exhibitions over local content emerged as a recurring concern for respondents across all three case studies. Highlighting the tendency for institutions to act, predominantly, as venues for travelling displays originating outside their region, the interviewees worried that their programs would be dominated by the cultural heritage of larger metropolitan centres (for whose audiences those exhibitions were originally developed). Inversely, opportunities to investigate and validate the cultural distinctiveness of communities in regional areas would be sidelined. As the art gallery and collections team leader at Lonehill remarked:

> I think rural communities are very hard on themselves. They see themselves as the poor cousins of the major cities. And they don't have to be. They have attributes that are unique that need to be related, and they have a part in the national story, and that needs to be told too.
>
> (team leader, art gallery and collections, Lonehill)

The same respondent argued that her institution's over-reliance on touring exhibitions reduced the possibilities for showcasing objects from the organisation's own collection:

> In this institution, when I arrived here, it revolved totally around touring product. Churn 'em in, churn 'em out. There was no major exhibition from the collection, and people in the community complained about not seeing the Drysdales, which are very much part of the community, or the Dupains, but just seeing the touring exhibitions.[6]
>
> (team leader, art gallery and collections, Lonehill)

In other words, the content and themes presented in travelling exhibitions were of limited relevance to the community, while artworks and objects with tangible links to the local region remained in storage.

At Westlands, the manager, collections officer and curator all conceded that the institution had a duty to compensate for infrequent changes to content in the permanent exhibition by delivering a greater number of temporary exhibitions dealing with local themes. However, as evident in the accounts provided below, this imperative was complicated by an imbalance in budget allocation for gallery versus museum temporary exhibitions. As a result, fewer financial and staff resources were available to conduct museum exhibition development:

> Under our current status, the museum curator would be the poor second cousin three times removed in terms of workload and in terms of the

budget. The museum has a budget – probably about $24–25,000 a year. The gallery has a budget of $150–160,000 a year for exhibitions.

(manager of Westlands)

We had a few museum shows that were curated in-house that probably weren't the best exhibitions that we've ever done, and there was a sense that they were like that because there was no time to do anything more.

(collections officer, museum and art gallery, Westlands)

As these extracts demonstrate, despite a stated commitment to producing an increased number of exhibitions using the organisation's own collections, insufficient funding and staffing for museum exhibition development resulted in what staff themselves perceived to be mediocre displays.

For members of the exhibitions team at Maunga Tapu, development of temporary exhibitions was hampered by the fact that, from the time of the organisation's establishment, there had been no plan to develop temporary exhibitions in-house. Correspondingly, responsibility for curatorial work was not clearly defined in the organisational structure, with a formal division drawn between the heritage collections team – responsible for cataloguing, research and collection documentation – and the exhibitions team, which focussed on facilities management and coordinating the calendar of travelling exhibitions. The exhibitions manager described the effects of this disjuncture, noting that exhibitions utilising objects from the organisation's own collection had usually only been developed when 'gaps' in the travelling exhibitions roster needed to be filled. Although these exhibitions proved worthwhile, the heritage collections team was not adequately staffed to take on these additional duties:

On an informal level, we've had a couple of people from collections develop exhibitions. That's not part of their job description, but they've done a fabulous job just actually using what we've got in-house and filling some gaps with some really cost-efficient and really engaging exhibitions. We've got to encourage that sort of thing more. But they've got a day job as well. Putting that sort of effort into an exhibition, which isn't part of their primary role, is a really hard thing to justify and places a lot of stress on them.

(manager, exhibitions, Maunga Tapu)

In this case, the separation of collection research and exhibition development roles seems at odds with conventional museum staffing structures, where

Process conflict 61

(at least ideally) original research of collections allows for exhibitions to evolve organically through the identification of culturally and locally significant themes and relationships between objects. In effect, the organisational structure at Maunga Tapu discouraged dialogue between museum professionals with rigorous knowledge of the collections and those with authority to initiate exhibition projects.

Interestingly, at both Westlands and Maunga Tapu, a disposition towards pre-packaged, travelling exhibitions, rather than temporary exhibitions curated in-house, demonstrates a disconnect between staff with knowledge of collections and the eventual public programs offered by these institutions. In the case of Westlands, the curator was responsible for both research and exhibition development, but, as discussed in a previous section of this chapter, in-depth knowledge of the museum collection remained unattainable due to his workload and the time-intensive nature of museum collection research.

Participants at Lonehill described similar circumstances. The art gallery and collections team leader complained about her organisation's reliance on travelling exhibition 'product,' highlighting that its value was restricted to superficial notions of financial efficiency, rather than community benefit:

> Well, if you are going to reduce administrative costs, then you probably will do the touring exhibitions that you just churn in and churn out every six weeks because you don't have to do any research. You don't have to do any interpretation of it. You don't have to relate it to the community because it isn't part of the community. So yes, you can do that. The contribution is [only an] administrative saving.
>
> (team leader, art gallery and collections, Lonehill)

Pressure to maintain a busy calendar of temporary exhibitions, imported from other institutions, did little to foster engagement around issues of local interest, identity and historical importance. As the curator at Westlands observed:

> We need to do our own shows. It is crucial. We can't bring in too many things [travelling exhibitions] because there are too many things that this display here is not telling us. . . . At the end of the day, I keep saying we need to curate more. There is no point in us simply being a venue. Being a 'venue' is attractive to a lot of people, in the sense that you just show things that pass through, and we have that role to play. But we are much, much more than that.
>
> (curator, museum and art gallery, Westlands)

62 *Process conflict*

Interpretation: 'It's the mediation thing, isn't it?'[7]

Issues relating to the interpretation of museum collections – the ways in which the meanings, values and relevance of objects are constructed and communicated within the museum context – are implicit in all of the themes considered within this chapter so far. In particular, the parameters according to which institutions select objects for inclusion in their collections, the ways and extent to which those objects are researched and documented, as well as points of access to collections (through permanent and temporary exhibitions, databases and so on) all play a role in determining how object meanings are understood by collection users. However, interpretation as a constitutive element of museum practice within converged institutions has not been explicitly considered so far. In the concluding part of the chapter, I therefore focus on the implications of convergence for interpretive processes through the accounts given by participants in the study.

Domain-based interpretive approaches

The integrity of specific library, archive, museum and gallery collection practices is maintained in institutions that retain a singular disciplinary focus. However, in cases of convergence – with their concomitant hybridisation of operational functions and blurring of staff responsibilities – differences in the way in which collection professionals from different disciplinary backgrounds conduct their roles come into sharp relief. In relation to museum collection research and public program development, participants remarked on the impact of discrepancies in ideas about interpretation and differences in the priority given to interpretive practice.

For respondents at Westlands and Lonehill, incompatibilities between museum, art gallery and library approaches to interpretation resulted in inconsistencies in the development and delivery of public programs. At Lonehill, where staff with a single area of professional expertise were assigned cross-domain roles following the convergence restructure, the library manager reflected on the period during which she had been responsible for museum, gallery and library collections. Explaining that her professional knowledge of the non-library areas increased gradually as she worked in her new position, she highlighted that a fundamental difference between museums and libraries is the relative importance placed on access versus interpretation of collections:

> It's really interesting, we explored this over time: librarians are very much about access – and I'm library-trained, but I have done up to a postgraduate certificate in museum studies, just to give me some

background – and I know museum people are about access as well, but librarians are about providing access to the collection, and that's their raison d'etre.... Interpretation is not as important to a librarian. Nor is that really detailed [collection] documentation.

(library manager, Lonehill)

A library's emphasis on making book stock available to the public as soon as possible elevates the importance of expedient cataloguing procedures. By contrast, the primary research often required for accessioning and documentation of museum objects, together with processes of interpretation (building thematic relationships between objects, composing exhibition texts and other publications, devising visual strategies for the presentation of collections, etc.), necessitates much slower 'progress' in workflow. One of the members of the heritage collections team at Maunga Tapu made specific reference to these differences, comparing the specific ways in which libraries and museums understand the role of interpretation in the service they provide to users:

> Yeah, it's the mediation thing, isn't it? Like, sure, we [the library] facilitate the lending of books that have information, [and] that will translate to knowledge, but the person takes that [book/resource] away and does all that stuff 'out there' and processes that however they may wish to – or not at all, if they don't bother reading the book or whatever. And then they come in, drop the book off, and that's all the library's required to do. Whereas the museum – and the way in which we try to facilitate [understanding] from our objects and the information around it, public programming and all of that – is incredibly labour-intensive by comparison.
>
> (heritage collections team member, Maunga Tapu)

In a sense, this respondent was drawing attention to the different points along the interpretative continuum that library items, as distinct from museum objects, become available to users.

By way of summarising the extracts above, it is worth quoting at length the former CEO of a national collections sector body, interviewed as part of this research. Speaking from her experience negotiating across the library, museum, archives and gallery domains, she offered her own synopsis of the different attitudes and practices of collection interpretation that are distinctive to each collecting area:

> The objects themselves can actually be considered in any way you want, managed in a converged way or not. The difference is in the attitude of the professional to that cultural material. I'm going to give you some stereotypes, but to me they are true. The traditionally trained

64 *Process conflict*

> librarian sits at the information desk. A customer – a user – comes forward (a potential reader, a user of the material) and says, 'Look, I'm chasing down this report. I can't find it anywhere.' The librarian says, 'Let me help you,' does some searching. . . . The librarian hasn't opened the covers, has just read the spine to make sure it's the right volume, and their day's work is absolutely fulfilled by having been able to put the document or artefact that the user wants into the user's hands, and they do not, in a sense, care what the user does with [it]. The librarian doesn't in any way interpret that material for the user. Whereas the museum curator or education officer or collection manager will be similarly thrilled at being able to match up a research enquiry with a real object, but they will also read the catalogue information and add to the information about that object by fleshing out the understanding of it in an interpretive way.
>
> (former senior staff member, national collections sector agency)

This respondent's ideas reflect the comments of the previously cited participants in outlining domain-based differences in the extent to which collections are interpreted for meaning. They also underscore the importance of particular professional skills and expertise on the 'end products' and end-user experiences delivered by different kinds of collecting institutions.

Interpreting across the domains

For many of the participants in this research, competing approaches to interpretation resulted in challenges to the sustainability of converged role descriptions.

At Westlands, respondents described the 'process conflict' that developed when individual staff members, whose previous expertise and experience were limited to either museums or the visual arts sector, were required to work across the two disciplinary fields. In particular, as the following two extracts demonstrate, disagreement around the appropriate level of interpretation for exhibitions, as well as uncertainties about catering appropriately to perceived differences in the expectations of museum versus gallery audiences, were common sources of tension and frustration for staff:

> Narrative revelation, rather than resolution – that's what the museum world needs to work in. But a lot of the art galleries don't have that narrative, and they don't want that narrative; they view anything that gets in the road of just seeing the artwork as almost anathema to it.
>
> (manager of Westlands)

And I know also that there's a tendency, for example, on [the manager's] part, with gallery shows, to have lots and lots of text because he comes from a museum and education background where interpretation and information is what people want. Whereas [the curator] is reluctant to do that because he comes from an art background where . . . you don't over-interpret, you let people work it out for themselves. So, there is a bit of a process conflict there, coming from different perspectives at something.

(collections officer, museum and art gallery, Westlands)

At Westlands, it was difficult for individual staff members to balance the contrasting demands produced by the time-intensive nature of museum collection research and exhibition development, as opposed to visual arts curatorial practices. The Westlands curator stressed the diminished sense of accomplishment produced by this situation. As the manager of that institution confirmed:

RESPONDENT: Well, the curators that we've had have . . . all been from fine arts backgrounds. So they are far more comfortable working within the gallery sphere, rather than the museum sphere. Museum shows are far more difficult to do.
INTERVIEWER: In what way?
RESPONDENT: They require a lot more research, they require a lot more time and they require a lot more material, in a sense. Whereas, within a regional arts base, you can have a couple of meetings with an artist, go to their studio and give them some advice or talk about what they're doing, get them to write an artist's statement for the floor sheet, and then the work comes in and you spend a few days arranging it. There's a lot of conceptual work in that, but it's not the sitting down and slogging through books and newspaper articles to find exactly who said what and when and to find objects to illustrate that story.

(manager of Westlands)

It became very difficult for staff to reconcile the different levels of significance attributed to the informational versus affective properties of museum collections in comparison to art gallery objects.

While respondents at Westlands were conscious of the limitations that switching between museum and gallery 'headspaces' placed on achieving efficiency and high standards across the institution's programs, there was a sense among employees that any attempts to improve the situation would be resisted by the local council. According to the centre coordinator, the primary concern for the council was to maintain (i.e. avoid increasing) the resource allocation to the institution even if this resulted in a gradual decline in the quality of its services:

> I think council's really happy that they have this great centre and there's really good feedback, and they just want it now to 'go' – so 'don't do anything fabulous that will impact on your staff, don't have more venue hire because we don't want to hear you say you need more staff, don't have more shows –just have the basic and don't make them fancy because we just want to say, ' "We have a great centre over there."' But they don't understand that to keep it going with the people over there – the industry is saying we've got to do these things and these new things are happening – and of course, professionally, they [the staff] want to be delivering the best. I think council just wants to have 'enough' – don't do too much, just do 'enough.'
>
> (centre coordinator, Westlands)

At both Westlands and Lonehill, the organisational structures created through convergence contrived to bring together professionally distinct library, museum and art gallery traditions for interpreting collections, producing complex and cross-disciplinary role descriptions beyond the training and experience of existing staff. With the reduced potential for museum collection interpretation in these scenarios, it could be argued that convergence failed to deliver on the fundamental promise of genuine cross-pollination of expertise, new contextual linkages between collections and enriched cultural experiences for audiences.

Conclusion: museum interpretive practices and convergence

This chapter has examined the effects of convergence on museum practices, underpinned by the assumption that structural changes to collecting organisations (including the configuration of management structures, funding arrangements, redefinition of position descriptions, the deployment and expectations placed on professional staff with particular disciplinary expertise, etc.) have the capacity to fundamentally alter the interpretive context for museum collections. I considered the ability of staff working with museum collections in converged institutional settings to perform professional museum work related to acquisitions and collection development, cataloguing and documentation, preservation, exhibitions and other interpretative activities. It is these activities that ultimately shape the quantity and quality of the information produced around collections, facilitating intellectual access to the diverse histories, cultural practices and community groups represented through collections and determining the potential for objects to be utilised in public programs.

Based on the findings from the case studies, it is clear that bringing disparate collections physically together and enabling communication between different collection specialists move converged GLAMs towards the rhetorical ideal of the interdisciplinary 'knowledge institution.' The integration of local studies collections with museums can certainly assist in the formation of research links between related objects, images and documents, thereby improving the ability to identify thematic connections across collections. Conversely, though, institution-wide budget models that neglect funding for new acquisitions can also stymie opportunities for strategic development of museum collections.

Indeed, the case studies demonstrate how various combinations of misaligned staff responsibilities, overambitious public programming goals and imbalanced distribution of resources within an organisation can neutralise advances to collection practice. As a case in point, in all three cases, the convergence restructure precipitated improvements to basic museum collection documentation through the instigation of formal collection policies and employment of professional staff. At the same time, significant backlogs in cataloguing and research of museum collections remained unresolved, staff were frustrated by their inability to conduct sustained collection research and the promise of creating thematic connections between collections via integrated digital databases had not been effectively realised.

Questions surrounding the net gain of convergence extend to exhibitions. The use of external contracted curators and short lead times for exhibition development characterised the set-up of new permanent display areas, leading to the installation of exhibitions with stilted narratives and limited relevance to the local community. Shortages in ongoing funding for exhibition renewal resulted in static permanent displays; staff members were unable to adequately modify these spaces to adapt to audience engagement needs. And while convergence provided greater variety and flexibility in the use of space for temporary exhibitions, respondents pointed out that the funding models of their institutions prioritised regular rotation of travelling displays rather than in-house development of exhibitions focussed on local content (which inevitably required labour-intensive primary research and documentation of collections). Over-reliance on touring exhibition 'product' therefore reduced institutions' ability to interpret the unique heritage of local regions and their populations. A clash of domain-based approaches to documentation methods and interpretation in a converged GLAM structure – so-called 'process conflict' – was also shown to have a potentially detrimental impact on museum research and exhibitions (especially when staff from non-museum backgrounds became responsible for museum collections).

Based on this analysis, there are a number of significant challenges to museum practice that appear to be specifically related to converged collection environments. First, all case studies provide examples of museums existing in parallel with other collecting areas (archives, local studies collections, art galleries, libraries, research centres), where an overall budget was split unevenly between these areas and their subsidiary functions. As a result, many respondents described chronic shortfalls in funding for basic museum activities such as accessioning, object research and significance assessment. Participants also noted that a greater share of resources was directed towards 'outward-facing' programs, such as a busy calendar of temporary displays comprised primarily of touring exhibitions developed elsewhere, rather than promoting the development of displays and public programs that utilised the institution's own collections. These circumstances compromised staff's capacity to devote adequate time to labour-intensive activities such as researching collections, perpetuating a pattern of comparatively superficial engagement with the collections and, subsequently, diminishing the range of opportunities for interacting with collections that could be made available to end users (local communities) down the line.

In this chapter, I have used the accounts of staff working with museum collections in converged institutions to scrutinise the benefits as well as threats to 'interpretive sustainability' at the granular level of collection documentation, research, narrative development and exhibition programs. But this is not the end of the story. As the interview extracts already indicate, day-to-day collection practice is nested within wider management contexts that shape individual staff interactions and responsibilities. In the following chapter, I therefore consider how organisational vision and goals, strategic planning, leadership, financial structures, the design of role descriptions and other administrative processes shape museum practice and collection meanings.

Notes

1 See Gibson, Morris and Cleeve 2007; Yarrow, Clubb and Draper 2008; Tanackovic and Badurina 2009; Bastian and Harvey 2012; Duff et al. 2013.
2 See Robinson 2018.
3 Retaining the anonymity of the institutions and respondents was a condition of the research on which this book is based. A description of each case study institution is available in Appendix 1. A summary of the scale and scope of each institution, together with details of the staff interviewed for this research, can be found in Appendix 2.
4 See Appendix 2.

5 The same problem extended to collection storage and preservation. Although respondents acknowledged that the increased public profile of their institutions (owing significantly to centrally located new facilities) meant that the council was obliged to provide resources for collection care, persisting shortages of storage space, preparation areas and provision of staff and budget for conservation of collections remained.
6 Reference to works by prominent Australian artists, painter Russell Drysdale (1912–1981) and photographer Max Dupain (1911–1992).
7 Heritage collections team member, Maunga Tapu, describing fundamental differences between library and museum approaches to collection documentation.

4 Mixed messages

Organisational structure and management of convergence

> *I actually haven't been able to find that definitive document or argument that says 'this is our vision, this is where we want to go.'*
>
> —group leader, cultural services, city council, Lonehill

How, if at all, can the administration of a cultural organisation influence the specialised work of professionals engaged in researching, interpreting and presenting museum objects? Although it is the collection documentation and curatorial activities of museum workers that generate the recognisable audience-facing outputs of collecting institutions – permanent and temporary exhibitions, educational programs, publications, public events and the like – these are in fact endpoints of an operational continuum that begins with, and continues to be animated by, an array of internal 'back-of-house' functions. As Conal McCarthy acknowledges in his introduction to *Museum Practice*, these 'hidden' activities form the basis of a 'functional process model' (2015, xxxv) comprising governance and management structures, strategic planning, the establishment of policy frameworks and allocation of financial and staff resources as well as the definition of specific roles and responsibilities. An analysis of the processual outcomes of interactions between human actors and organisational frameworks has the capacity to produce a 'practice theory' of hybridised collecting institutions that is theoretically informed (via, for example, the epistemological concepts discussed in Chapter 2 of this book) while remaining grounded in the 'street-level' study of human action and its consequences for collection interpretation.[1]

Having examined how specialised disciplinary approaches to collection interpretation are reconfigured, cross-pollinate and/or compete in converged institutions in the previous chapter, this section of the book explores

Mixed messages 71

the extent to which higher-level strategic realignment and new bureaucratic structures produce a flow-on effect on collection-level work. I consider how institution-wide changes to administration, funding and structure, together with the strategic goals and leadership of an organisation, can impact (or interfere with) the ways in which collections are documented, researched and presented to visitors.

These findings complement and build on those presented in the previous chapter. The staff interviews demonstrate how the broad institutional frameworks for convergence produce particular conditions for museum practice. Areas of management and administration, including how resources are allocated, expectations regarding staff performance and the redesign of individual job descriptions, combine in interesting ways to dictate both the extent and context of staff engagement with objects and each other, with surprising consequences for their ability to explore the meanings of collections.

Articulating the concept of convergence

A logical starting point for this chapter is to begin with an analysis of what the interviews tell us about how a conceptual rationale for convergence was communicated to staff at each organisation. The research revealed a mixture of perceived justifications for convergence – which I detail below – ranging from the philosophical to the purely pragmatic. Together with the different iterations of convergence adopted across the case studies, the variety of explanations provided for the restructures positioned the priorities of converged institutions across a wide spectrum of end goals. For museum collections in particular, uncertainty around organisational vision resulted in varying degrees of emphasis on the importance of interpretative museum practice.

A holistic view of culture

Agreement about the rationale for convergence was rare among participants in the study, but perhaps the only point of consensus for several respondents, across all three cases, was the idea that convergence broadly makes sense as a concept of uniting diverse forms of cultural expression. As I have outlined in Chapter 1, the idea that all kinds of collections, regardless of their physical form and organisation, are physical manifestations of culture is the humanistic principle at the heart of many arguments for domain integration. From this perspective, typological distinctions or boundaries created by the different collecting traditions artificially compartmentalise materials that are intrinsically linked. Some respondents recognised the potential to understand the significance of any collection object in numerous ways and therefore that convergence provides an opportunity for the inherent relationships between objects and collections to be made explicit. The perceived joint purpose of locally embedded collecting institutions was referenced by a number of participants. Some respondents at Lonehill recognised that museums, libraries with local studies collections and archives shared a common purpose in maintaining and responding to the heritage of their communities. Staff members at Maunga Tapu noted that the previously independent museum already held archival and historical photograph collections normally associated with libraries, so it made sense to integrate those services formally. One respondent at Lonehill recognised the potential of convergence in making thematic connections between collections visible through integrated public programs, simultaneously enabling greater staffing efficiency in that department:

> An important consideration for us, and it relates very much to the audience development, was the potential for programming across library and museum services. The way the structure ended up going initially was across the gallery as well, but we just thought, in terms of programming for various demographics and educational services, there were so many advantages to having one team that was able to program across all our cultural services and facilities.
>
> (library manager, Lonehill)

A member of the learning and outreach team at Lonehill spoke of the benefits of designing children's educational programs to incorporate engagements with library books and thematically related objects in the museum display in a single visit, thereby reinforcing learning outcomes. With traditionally lower visitation than their library counterparts, the museum components of the convergences at Lonehill and Maunga Tapu were seen to be the main beneficiaries of the potential for audience crossover.

Improving access to cultural amenities

It was the prevalence of pragmatic, rather than philosophical, rationales for convergence that predominated the accounts of respondents across the three institutions. In all the case studies, the desire to create a central cultural precinct as a vibrant community focal point and tourism hub – often epitomised by investment in 'iconic' architecture – featured prominently as an incentive in pursuing convergence. As one staff member at Westlands put it:

> I guess it was seen as just a common-sense approach . . . because they [local councils] are all for precincts now and having these things in one

place. It just came out of a need; they weren't going to have all these [separate] places and say we are going to have an art gallery over there and a museum over here.

(centre coordinator, Westlands)

Respondents in every case study conceded that existing museum, library, gallery and archive facilities required upgrading before convergence was mooted, so the idea of centrally located and integrated facilities simultaneously addressed the need for infrastructure renewal and improved visitor access.

Finally, one respondent at Maunga Tapu discussed the increasing pervasiveness of digital technology as direct competition to collecting institutions as information providers, envisaging convergence as a way of responding to user demands for greater information access by uniting collections as sources of 'knowledge':

> My feeling is that in ten or twenty years' time, we're going to look back at the idea of converging and think that was based on foresight because I think we're going to be forced to become more of a singular institution. The idea of a 'knowledge centre' is the critical concept for me. . . . We've got competition from the virtual world, and a surprising amount of people trust the internet.
>
> (manager, exhibitions, Maunga Tapu)

The same respondent predicted a shift in the professional roles of librarians, curators and other collection professionals from custodians to 'mediators of knowledge,' implying that collecting institutions would embrace a modified concept of curatorship modelled on helping users piece together information from numerous disparate sources to create their own meaning, rather than offering subject-specific expertise. Given the amount of recent international literature concerning the impact of digital technologies in creating the expectation of instantaneous, 'democratic' and unhindered access to information among users, the absence of this consideration among all but one of the interview participants was surprising.

A response to funding opportunities

Overwhelmingly, the most prominent justification for convergence provided by respondents in the research was pecuniary, rather than philosophical. Many participants in the research perceived both funding incentives and the promise of cost savings for local councils as the primary drivers for convergence.

On a number of occasions throughout her interview, a senior member of staff at Lonehill referred to the connection between state government grants and the decision to converge at her organisation, explaining how the availability of funding for convergence projects had skewed the form of restructuring undertaken at the institution:

> At that stage, we were also thinking about operating as a co-located [facility] – we were in that mode of planning for a new library and museum – and again, because there were funding opportunities available for some elements of 'convergence,' we started exploring it . . . funding was prevalent for anything that had the word 'converged' in it . . . [and] we were successful with a grant and employed a collection manager across our library, our local studies, our museum collection and our visual arts collection.
>
> (library manager, Lonehill)

Notably, the amount of designated convergence funding allocated to the Lonehill project amounted to only a small fraction of the total capital works and administrative costs. It is therefore surprising that a relatively small amount of state government funding provided enough incentive to get convergence over the line as the preferred organisational model for local governments seeking to redevelop their cultural amenities. In addition, neither state government grants nor local government allocations made adequate provision for recurrent operational costs of converged institutions, including staffing and building maintenance. As such, converged organisations became 'locked in' to an operating model and physical infrastructure without the security of long-term financial support.

Perhaps the cost efficiencies that local governments anticipated to gain through the converged model supressed questions about the ongoing funding sustainability of the resulting institutions. Respondents across all three case studies indicated that the expectation of lower expenditure – especially in the form of so-called 'economies of scale,' shared building costs, reduced duplication of resources and facilities (office space, toilets, parking, etc.) and reduction of staff numbers – provided a persuasive argument to local governments wishing to implement convergence, albeit at the expense of developing a rigorous conceptual rationale for the restructure:

> In relation to convergence, they liked the idea of that. Certainly, it can be sold to council in different ways. One of the ways that it was sold was about effective use of resources.
>
> (museum and social history coordinator, Lonehill)

INTERVIEWER: Do you know what the rationale was behind the idea to combine the various functions of this cultural centre?
RESPONDENT: Money.

(manager of Westlands)

I think a cynical person would say it was purely a way of combining administrative resources. It may have seemed to have made economic sense on some level because we're funded by the local council, and they're always looking at ways of working more efficiently.

(manager, exhibitions, Maunga Tapu)

The community services director, at the city council, responsible for Westlands emphasised that convergence provided the only mechanism by which all the component organisations could retain professional staff:

Obviously, we've got the economies of scale too. We couldn't have had a museum off at another site and duplicated that and had two managers.... And obviously, if it had been split, it would have been to the detriment of – saying this facility's going to have a collections officer, this one isn't. Or, this one's going to have an education officer and this one isn't.

(community services director, city council, Westlands)

As outlined by the CEO of an NSW museum and gallery agency interviewed for this study, the prospect that convergence could deliver financial savings to local governments – who are responsible for multiple cultural facilities – often trumped any philosophical justification for restructuring. According to the collections and exhibitions officer at Lonehill, the attention given to crafting appropriate staff structures or recruiting adequately qualified staff was not always equal to the emphasis on achieving cost savings, sometimes resulting in the loss of experienced staff:

I think the idea with convergence was to take away the art gallery person and the museum person and get one person to do both jobs. They advertised that job at the same rate as the previous curatorial job, and the curator at that time said, 'I'm out of here! I'll take the redundancy, thank you very much – I'm not going to do two institutions' worth of work for the same wage.'

(collections and exhibitions officer, Lonehill)

In the end, a number of respondents across the case studies acknowledged that financial efficiency is problematic as a long-term expectation of hybrid institutions. Where the emphasis on cost reduction dominates restructuring processes, converged organisations lack the focus and resources to consistently deliver innovative and engaging services and programs.

No reason[2] *– the absence of a vision*

As I have just outlined, respondents in this study identified three core rationales for the emergence of the convergence trend in NSW. First, a small minority of participants cited the possibility of combining diverse forms of cultural material – and the subsequent potential to creatively exploit relationships between those cultural forms – as an overarching goal. Others referenced improvements in access to collections, extending the idea of co-located cultural facilities and 'precincts', as a significant factor. Finally, of those who were able to articulate a clear rationale, a number pointed to local government expectations that convergence would result in financial efficiencies as the overriding motivation.

Unambiguously, however, lack of a strong conceptual vision for convergence was identified by staff across all three cases. Respondents at Lonehill speculated that the convergence arose as a form of managerial reorganisation – a 'bureaucratic model' where the possibility of developing greater access to disparate collection resources was only a secondary by-product:

> I think that was there [the information-sharing rationale], but probably only after a decision was made that we were going to be together. That's when we started exploring those convergence opportunities – after the decision was made that we would be together.
> (library manager, Lonehill)

At Lonehill, the group leader for cultural services (a city council role) conceded, 'I actually haven't been able to find that definitive document or argument that says "this is our vision, this is where we want to go"' – a sentiment echoed by the manager of Westlands:

> I think there might have been one paper raised about the theoretical implications of it, but I think it was more of a discussion paper, and it never really ironed out what the final thing would look like. It didn't lay out a path as to how the new centre was going to act, what it was going to feel like and what it was going to do. It was very much about what it was going to look like: where was the museum, where was the art gallery and so forth.
> (manager of Westlands)

Echoing their counterparts at Lonehill, participants at Maunga Tapu described ongoing uncertainty about the role of their institution and the purpose of convergence. A member of the exhibitions team complained that the restructured institution's identity remained ambiguous, saying, 'It's not very clear what the institution is trying to be. Our mission statement is basically meaningless as far as I can tell, and it's laden with policy-speak.' His team manager, concerned about the organisation's ability to communicate effectively to its users, similarly stated,

> I think we really struggle ourselves to articulate what we are as a whole. I think we still operate as a library and a museum and a research centre. Which is disappointing, I guess, that after eight years people working here still can't fully explain to outsiders what we are as a whole . . .
> . . . We don't have a vision. You know, if you ask anyone here what [Maunga Tapu] is, you're going to get a hundred thousand different answers, but you're not going to get that singular vision that makes sense. And until we get that, we can't sell ourselves to the community very well.
> (manager, exhibitions, Maunga Tapu)

According to these staff, an unresolved vision was symptomatic of poor planning by management and other decision-makers involved in the restructuring of the institutions. Moreover, the absence of a clear set of aspirational, unified goals undermined efforts by staff to strategically align their daily work priorities, internal collaborations and public programs. The result was a splintered workplace culture, where individual units compensated for the absence of a coherent strategic vision by establishing their own objectives, regardless of the activities of other groups and sometimes in direct contradiction to the ideal of cross-domain and cross-functional integration:

> In regard to that lack of leadership that we've been talking about – that lack of vision for the whole institution – what it has required is for individual teams, or even individuals themselves, to find meaning behind their own working strategy. We've said, 'Right, well, we are going to prioritise this, and whatever else is going on out there, we'll just try to forge ahead and do some good stuff based on what we've identified as being important for us.' That's not at the exclusion of others or wanting to be different to them. It's just the only way of looking forward.
> (heritage collections team member, Maunga Tapu)

Ironically, where converged institutions remain conceptually adrift as a result of the largely economic rationales that have driven their establishment, teams and even individual workers can become more isolated, creating surrogate missions and strategies that suit the purposes of their own department or area. Especially in cases where reductions have been made in staff numbers (or the responsibilities of existing staff have been expanded as a result of the convergence), staff focus becomes more 'siloed,' stymieing potential for collaboration and eroding trust between departments. The resulting frustration of some staff at Maunga Tapu was summed up well by a member of the heritage collections team:

> I think that one of the things that rides us off is . . . there is no real sense of direction. Like, the heritage team is working on updating our collections plan to give us priorities over the next period of time, but we have no idea if – and I don't believe they [the exhibitions team] have an exhibitions plan. Where are they going? And how do we fit into providing material that's required for forthcoming shows? What are the kinds of [thematic] threads that they're trying to promote through their programming? There isn't any strong articulation of that, which creates a whole lot of other issues.
>
> (heritage collections team member, Maunga Tapu)

Cross-disciplinary cooperation at Maunga Tapu was initiated by staff, rather than by the institution's leadership. The conceptual benefits of convergence in uniting thematically connected collections were being realised only sporadically, depending on the goodwill shown by individual staff, rather than a well-articulated vision, collaborative workplace culture or conducive organisational structure.

Leadership and management issues

The previous section detailed how respondents at the case study organisations described the institutional vision and rationales for convergence (or lack thereof). Extracts from the interviews highlight the mixed messages and frustrating lack of conceptual foundations that characterised the experience of convergence for many of the participants in this research. But the idea of convergence and its operational realisation is also mediated through a framework of management structures, as well as planning processes, that establishes strategies and mechanisms for the day-to-day functioning of institutions and their staff. This section focuses on these administrative areas and considers the role and enactment of museum practices in these contexts.

Challenges in implementing change

A significant theme that developed through the analysis of the interviews concerned the planning and implementation of change in converged institutions and associated issues of leadership, organisational restructuring and sustainability.

Following discussion of institutional vision, the need for strong leadership through the change process was clearly expressed by a number of participants, primarily as a means of driving and sustaining collaboration across various collections and professional disciplines. Commitment to the idea of collaboration needed to be demonstrated by all levels of management as 'holders of the vision.' In reference to Maunga Tapu in particular, the CEO of the district council described the need for strong and inspirational leadership as a goal that had yet to be fully realised at the institution. Without it, divisive competition between sections was likely to prevail, inevitably undermining fruitful collaboration and hybridisation:

> I always find it really easy for people to intellectually embrace a vision, but the test is actually to see how they behave. I see it all the time, even in my own executive. We will intellectually embrace the idea of a certain culture in our organisation and a certain style of leadership, and then you watch them settle back into their old patterns of behaviour. And they don't even know they're doing it. So I think that's a great challenge in convergence – the way in which the staff are led and brought together . . .
>
> . . . Cracking the whole potential of convergence takes a lot of time, strong leadership, the selection of the right people and someone to uphold that vision and not let it go. I think it's very easy to slip back . . . into old behaviours.
>
> (CEO, district council, Maunga Tapu)

A number of respondents from Lonehill acknowledged that poor planning for the convergence, combined with insufficient communication to staff about the rationale for the changes and the radical reconfiguration of job descriptions to fit a converged organisational model, left many employees feeling disenfranchised and confused about their new roles. One senior staff member observed:

> I think people were spread very thin across areas . . . and there was a lack of change management, people put into positions without the appropriate skills or training or support. Disgruntled staff, lack of motivation, a whole heap of things happening, and it wasn't ideal.
>
> (library manager, Lonehill)

The resulting resistance to change among some staff sabotaged the potential for the idea of convergence to be adopted fully and enthusiastically.

80 *Mixed messages*

At Westlands, respondents observed that the lack of museum representation in the initial design of the converged organisational structure had created a legacy of disadvantage for the museum collection. The council's move towards a hybrid institution initially saw the promotion of the previous gallery manager to the overall leadership of the new organisation. There was limited consultation with existing staff about the distribution of resources across operational functions. Some employees who had previously worked with and were passionate about the museum collection were redeployed, leaving no museum staff to advocate for its preservation and interpretive requirements. The local studies officer – one of two staff who had overseen the museum collection prior to the convergence – described her ongoing resentment about the abrupt and non-consultative change process that had characterised the restructure:

> Then we had a meeting with the manager, who rarely had a meeting with us, and I said to her, 'My contract's coming up next month,' and she said, 'Oh, you're not going to be here [at the museum] anymore.' I said, 'Beg your pardon?!' She said, 'You're going to the library,' and I was gobsmacked because I'd never heard of it before, and I was about to go on holiday to New Zealand. At 4.20, the director from here [the library] rings up and says, 'When you come back from New Zealand, you're coming straight back here,' and that's how it was. So, I did pack up as much as I could. I rang my husband bawling my eyes out.
>
> (local studies officer, Westlands)

At Maunga Tapu, a number of employees felt that the integrated institutional structure had been imposed on them. Feeling disassociated from the decision-making process, few felt ownership of the idea of convergence, perpetuating the tendency for staff to revert to less collaborative ways of working.

Genuinely 'converged' leadership?

For many respondents, the leadership of a converged institution represented a crucial starting point for setting the tone for collaboration, participation and validation of professional skills across the organisation. For this reason, successes or failures in strategic planning and restructuring, as well as systemic problems in communication and collaboration, were seen by many to stem from the professional background and particular managerial approach of institutional leaders.

The ability of management to appreciate and equally value different collection areas and the expertise of their staff was identified as key to effective leadership. However, respondents across all three case studies expressed concern about shifting management goals and persisting biases that pit one collecting area against another. At Lonehill and Maunga Tapu, a major concern was the extent to which the professional background of the manager or leader influenced the direction and priorities of the facility overall. Members of the museum collections team at Maunga Tapu were emphatic that the director's partiality in favour of the library component of the institution resulted in under-resourcing of the museum:

> I think one of the major problems with convergence as a model is that generally you'll have one director, or manager, and as they come from a particular background, how fair or reasonable is it to expect that they have the same level of knowledge and passion for two or more aspects of a business?
>
> The reality is, from my point of view, I don't really care how the library staff [members] do what they do as long as they do what they do and the customers are happy. Whereas, from my point of view, what I have a passion for is museums, and that's what I like to put my energy into. So, I don't see how it can work with a manager who has knowledge and passion with regard to one aspect of the business. How does the other aspect not lose out?
>
> (heritage collections team member, Maunga Tapu)

At Lonehill, a member of the exhibitions team speculated that converged institutions required specialist managers with experience in overseeing collaboration across multiple collecting areas. At Maunga Tapu, the manager of exhibitions called for the establishment of a new job title to reflect the holistic responsibilities of converged administration: 'sort of like having a creative director who knows about the cultural sector but not necessarily a "librarian" or a "museums person"' – in other words, a leader who could transcend disciplinary boundaries to provide an inclusive, collaborative vision for the organisation's wider contribution to culture.

Planning and organisational design

According to numerous participants in the study, lack of clarity around institutional purpose and perceived favouritism on the part of management were compounded by utopian organisational design, including role descriptions and reporting mechanisms that were out of touch with the demands of everyday professional practice in galleries, archives, museums and libraries. As funders and governing bodies, local councils were perceived as having limited understanding of the cultural mission of collecting institutions and therefore poorly equipped to devise a workplace that effectively responded to the functional complexity of hybrid institutions.

A significant complaint, articulated by staff members as well as representatives of collections sector advisory bodies, was that local government emphasised the construction of monumental buildings to house newly converged institutions over and above the development of effective organisational structures and long-term operational funding provisions.[3] As the library manager from Lonehill pointed out, the local council in that region had very little involvement with the management of the museum or gallery prior to the convergence, so it was only after the restructure that the council became more aware of the daily activities of those organisations. At Westlands – where the converged facility fell under the council's department of community services – employees expressed frustration at the council's ignorance of their specialised activities:

> I believe that people don't know what you do. I remember people saying, 'What do all those people do over there?' They think a truck just pulls up and they just hang pictures on a wall. They don't see planning or programming or collection-based items or education and outreach. People don't see what's happening.
> ... The general council, as in the executive, wider afield, they have no idea about what the gallery or the museum do.
>
> (centre coordinator, Westlands)

A similar set of circumstances evolved at Lonehill, where the group leader, cultural services (a city council role), acknowledged that the publicised opening date for the institution had compressed the planning process for converged staffing structure, resulting in a series of subsequent and further destabilising restructures as the operational needs of the new institution became apparent. In the case of Maunga Tapu, the district council's CEO, who had been the first manager of the converged institution, recalled how the council had ignored professional advice and wilfully underestimated the running costs of the new organisation:

> I remember saying to them, 'We are going to need these sorts of staff, and it's going to cost us this much money.' The answer was, 'No, you're not going to get that.' My answer was, 'Well, why are we building this thing if we don't have the budget we need to run it?'
>
> (CEO, district council, Maunga Tapu)

According to this respondent, the district council feared that the project would lose community support if realistic estimates of its running costs were acknowledged and made public from the outset. Effectively, this handicapped the institution, creating a staffing structure and budgets that were insufficient to allow the organisation to function successfully.

Across the case studies, capacity to develop engaging, locally appropriate programs was compromised by councils that were unaware of the complexities and professional standards of collection work. Respondents complained that their institutions were chronically under-resourced, with employees regularly working outside the 'official' structure to assist with staffing shortfalls in other sections. The necessity of multitasking, combined with intensive schedules for the delivery of exhibitions and public programs, meant that the priorities of staff shifted constantly, leaving respondents frustrated that tasks were sometimes not achieved to a high enough standard or were left incomplete:

> When it comes to the team that [the exhibitions coordinator] works with, that's the exhibitions team, so he's responsible for installing any exhibitions, moving artwork around, accepting exhibitions from outside and touring them around. He's got a 'team' of himself and one other person as well. For either 'team' to achieve anything, you have to use someone from the other team. So, each time you take somebody out of this team to do the other team's work, this team does nothing. It actually becomes a negative process because you are constantly being taken away from work that needs to be done systematically. It's one of my biggest frustrations.
> (collections and exhibitions officer, Lonehill)

As the CEO of a museum and gallery peak body in NSW concluded in his interview, the preoccupation of local councils with the development of iconic cultural facilities without factoring in realistic ongoing operational costs was a pattern repeated in relation to many convergence projects:

> There's always been an issue there about the current costs and staffing and programming, and the councils have never really bitten that bullet. But they've always had that 'edifice complex' thing.
> (CEO, NSW museum and gallery peak body)

In these ways, investment by local governments in high-profile new buildings, lack of a clearly articulated strategic vision and insufficient operating budgets combined to undermine the potential success of the convergence model.

New roles and expectations

The promise of professional cross-pollination and the sharing of skills across domain boundaries is regarded as a cornerstone of the convergence model. The ability of employees to pool their experience and build expertise across disciplines is seen as an important stepping stone towards the goals of integrated programming and innovative use of collections. And indeed, respondents across all case studies acknowledged that the convergence model had enabled greater communication between the various sections of their institutions in a number of different ways.

In the context of formal communication, the establishment of regular cross-departmental, cross-disciplinary meetings raised awareness of the variety of their activities, streamlining programming schedules to improve audience development. Many of the respondents across case studies also highlighted benefits to informal communication brought on by convergence. Participants at Maunga Tapu described a shared appreciation for other collection areas and the specialist skills of colleagues. The formal integration of collecting institutions into local government administrations also created new channels of communication between collections staff and council employees. In the context of museum practice, the ability to access professional staff from diverse collecting areas, with their specialist knowledge about available research materials and local history, held out the promise of enriched museum collection documentation, expedited and enhanced exhibition development processes and simplified delivery of thematically linked programs to audiences.

Nevertheless, for all its potential benefits, numerous respondents also described the obligation to participate in an unnecessarily complex and hierarchical management system as a barrier to efficiency. A number of specialist staff at Lonehill found that the converged reporting structure made it difficult to obtain consensus for innovative (or domain-specific) projects. Instead, ideas for new programs or exhibitions could be diluted through iterative meetings, complicating natural workflows and undermining the authority of specialist staff in decision-making situations:

> The people who actually were the creative thinkers and could easily put an exhibition together and had some really fantastic ideas weren't allowed to do it to full fruition. So, everything had to go to 'committee,' and you'd just get debated out of the room.
> (group leader, cultural services, city council, Lonehill)

In combination with the pressure to deliver cost efficiencies, insufficient resources for ongoing operations and poorly planned organisational and reporting structures, the implementation of new role descriptions produced varying degrees of confusion and stress at all the case study sites. Among the concerns expressed by respondents were reductions of staff numbers to achieve financial rationalisation, the allocation of roles to staff members who were not qualified for the work and even the establishment of 'converged' role descriptions as a tool for achieving staff redundancies. As the cultural development officer at Lonehill admitted, the implications of poorly designed roles extended beyond the ability of staff to do their jobs successfully, thwarting the institution's capacity to deliver important programs:

> There were lots of opportunities that were missed because there either was a team of people who could have done it but it wasn't their role or they didn't have the time to do it or the skills. Or, we just fumbled through without going through that process.
> (group leader, cultural services, city council, Lonehill)

At Lonehill, the initial restructure created management positions overseeing all collection areas simultaneously, placing staff with only one area of expertise in control of library, museum and gallery services. As one senior library employee who had originally assumed one of these managerial roles remarked:

> I didn't get staff. There wasn't a curator. There was no one from the museum to come under me. I could get a few technicians from the gallery to come under me, but there was no museum staff. I didn't get any extra staff when my position expanded because council wasn't sure how big a success this would be and what was going to be required when you opened a facility like this.
> (information and library collections coordinator, Lonehill)

Likewise, accounts offered by participants at Westlands emphasised the untenable scope of converged roles that straddled gallery, museum and community arts centre responsibilities. The manager at Westlands described maintaining a calendar of over 30 temporary exhibitions each year as 'maniacal,' while the curator (with a background in the visual arts but responsible for both museum and gallery displays) repeatedly described the difficulties in achieving adequate rigour in research of the museum collection and subsequent exhibition development:

> There's a number of issues because being curator of both institutions means that your time is non-existent. So, it's the pressures of making

sure a museum show is rigorous but at the same time done in a timely manner. There are tremendous problems in that. It's wanting to give that side of things [exhibition development] more time and at the same time keep everything else afloat.

(curator, museum and art gallery, Westlands)

The Westlands centre coordinator observed that staff members were reaching the point of complete exhaustion attempting to maintain professional standards in their work. In particular, the institution had no capacity to research and develop its own travelling exhibitions as a result of the extreme time pressure experienced by the staff:

> It is overwhelming sometimes! It's a lot of people going that extra mile, probably to the point where they just go, 'I'm not doing that anymore'. . . I don't know whether [the manager] knows how to fix where we are, unless we start putting down overtime or somehow showing [how much extra work we are doing].
> . . . Certainly, curation-wise, they can't above, or in front, of everything just say, 'Oh, I'm going to put a bit more time into touring a show.' I mean, it's just impossible. At the moment, there is no way they can tour a show because they can't [even] get what we've planned done.

(centre coordinator, Westlands)

What these examples illustrate is how the supposed organisational 'efficiency' of a converged framework, where formerly specialist roles were broadened to include a range of collecting areas and activities, created artificially high expectations of individuals assigned to those roles. The requirement for disciplinary knowledge and professional experience across multiple collecting fields was not made explicit, allowing the appointment of staff members who specialised in only a single collection area. Furthermore, the practicalities of fulfilling such broad duties proved unmanageable for many staff. In combination, respondents perceived that these factors had a detrimental effect on the amount and quality of collection research, exhibitions and collection development.

Cross-disciplinarity: an achievable goal?

Across the three case studies, many respondents agreed that convergence had introduced exciting potential for upskilling at their institutions. For a number of participants, convergence signalled opportunities for individual staff to 'step outside the old boundaries'[4] of their professional areas and experiment with alternative approaches to collections. However, these opportunities were missed through a lack of formal support for professional development and sharing of expertise. Some respondents observed that staff needed to establish mentorship and professional networks on their own, while others explained how, once installed in converged roles, they had had to personally take the initiative in organising additional training to overcome 'gaps' in their knowledge (or that they wished to do so but did not have the time). With a role encompassing both the museum and visual arts collections, the Westlands curator underscored the practical difficulties entailed in pursuing further professional training:

> I do feel that I would be doing the museum a slight disservice if I didn't do it [cataloguing, exhibition development, etc.] properly. I'm not even sure if I know what 'properly' is. I just feel a discomfort with... I don't feel resistant to it. I feel it's something I would love to jump into and really explore, but I'm conscious of the time that will take, and it would probably take a lot of my own time.
>
> (curator, museum and art gallery, Westlands)

Significantly, this staff member, whose training and previous experience were exclusively visual arts–based, was expected to function effectively across both the gallery and museum aspects of his role. While his commitment to the job remained intact, his confidence as a collection professional had been eroded through the lack of support to undertake the training he felt was necessary to effectively perform his role, leading to insecurity and self-doubt.

Across all three cases, participants highlighted lack of time and the absence of institutional frameworks for professional development as barriers to the extension and 'cross-fertilisation' of professional skills. One significant problem related to the time pressures created by understaffed organisations attempting to fulfil busy exhibition and programming commitments. In these situations, staff members who needed to improve their knowledge did not have the time to undertake further studies or to engage deeply with the collections outside of their area of expertise, with clear consequences for the management and interpretation of those collections. As the manager at Westlands noted when describing the processes of exhibition development at his organisation:

> Especially with the current curator, being from a fine arts background, he works much more efficiently and effectively within the sphere of

art. If you go over to the museum, it is clearly harder for him to wrap his head around it.

(manager of Westlands)

Noting the curator's reluctance to undertake museum exhibition development, the collections officer observed that the heavy workload on staff was compounded by the need for employees other than the curator to take up responsibility for displays:

> So, a lot of the museum shows are falling to other staff members because [the curator] didn't really want to do them. It wasn't his area of interest. It became a problem of whatever kind of background you brought to your position meant that you didn't necessarily attack the gallery and the museum with the same vigour and the same interest as you would if you were just a gallery curator or just a museum curator.
>
> (collections officer, museum and art gallery, Westlands)[5]

Staff members professional bias played a significant role in dictating the overall scope of a converged institution's activities. At Westlands, staff preferences resulted in the institution's overall programs becoming disproportionately weighted in favour of gallery exhibitions. It was clear that staff doubted the viability of converged curatorial roles and would have preferred a collaborative framework that allowed for specialists to focus and build on their established areas of expertise.

From converged role descriptions given to staff who specialised in only one collection area to the dilution of professional quality and neglect of certain collection tasks, many respondents highlighted ways in which an idealistic model of convergence had been imposed on their institutions without fully taking into account the effects on collection work and public programs. As the library manager at Lonehill explained:

> Our very first model of convergence went across the library, the museum and the gallery, and in a way a lot of us, including myself, were totally out of our depth. . . . [Responsibility for] the exhibition area, for someone who was library-trained and halfway through a museum course, was really not a great move. Basically, people like myself were put into positions without the experience and skills. And OK, I upskilled a lot, and it was great in some ways and incredibly challenging, but we were riding on a wave, and things were neglected as a result.
>
> (library manager, Lonehill)

The parts that remained 'neglected' were the aspects of museum and gallery work potentially invisible to someone coming from an exclusively library background: the ability to critically evaluate the cultural significance of individual collection items, creating thematic linkages between objects, pursuing the acquisition of important artefacts and building relationships with potential collection donors, performing time-intensive research of the collections and developing locally relevant exhibitions. Respondents across the case studies reinforced this perspective, identifying the expectation that an individual employee can be equally specialised across all collection areas as both idealistic and unrealistic.

At the time this research took place, there were no tertiary or other professional education courses in Australia training collection professionals for work in converged institutions. In this regard, the reformulation of role descriptions and organisational structures according to the converged framework was set up to falter. Its introduction as an institutional and professional model before the emergence of enough appropriately trained and experienced staff undercut the capacity of employees to effectively perform cross-disciplinary roles and harness the potential to create innovative programs across diverse collection holdings.

An interesting insight was provided by the former manager of Maunga Tapu, who unambiguously expressed the need to maintain excellence within the individual collections and associated professional fields that were combined in converged institutional structures:

> To have an excellent integrated service, we needed to have excellent component parts, in terms of our professional knowledge and skills.... I was very clear that we needed to build the reputation of both the library and the museum activities in their own sectors to have any chance of succeeding in saying that the integrated offer was something where the whole was greater than the sum of its parts. The parts have to be excellent, and if the whole is greater than the sum of its parts, you would expect it to be fabulous.
>
> (former manager of Maunga Tapu)

It is worth noting that this respondent stopped short of articulating precisely how specific professional areas – even when functioning at what might be considered 'optimal' levels – would collaborate to achieve an institution valued as a 'knowledge centre' that exceeded the expectations of co-located, but essentially independent, services. The evidence suggests that the bureaucratic breakdown of disciplinary boundaries was not accompanied by a new model of 'converged' professional identity and practices, once again pointing to shortcomings in leadership and strategic vision for convergence. The mechanisms for achieving a conceptually integrated model of convergence remained to be adequately planned, implemented and explained to staff.

With individual staff gravitating towards their original area of specialisation and 'siloed' work habits, the converged institutions under study remained at risk of disintegration. As indicated by the manager of Westlands, this placed an additional burden on senior management to sustain their organisation's focus on convergence and collaboration:

> One of the board members asked how we measure our success – 'How do you rate that? Is it just bums on seats or is it something more?' I said: 'Bums on seats,' is one way, but the 'something more' is that, at this stage of convergence, we haven't torn ourselves apart. That is successful! I think, in other institutions, they haven't been able to do that.
>
> (manager of Westlands)

Morale and job satisfaction

As many of the interview extracts reproduced here indicate, the emotional responses of staff subject to convergence were a significant influence on the attitudes they brought to their work and collaborations, with reciprocal impacts on professional practices and productivity. Many participants referred to a 'situational frustration' within their roles, resulting from overwork and uncertainty in regard to cross-disciplinary responsibilities. While a number of participants did express satisfaction with their job descriptions, it would not be exaggerating to say that stress, cynicism and, in some cases, despondency permeated many respondents' descriptions of their experiences working within a converged setting.

The very general nature of converged role descriptions proved particularly troublesome at Lonehill, where some employees felt insecure in their ability to perform their roles or failed to take full ownership of their work. Lonehill's cultural services group leader – a role similar to that of the managers in the other case studies – clearly outlined these issues in her accounts of the convergence restructure:

> There were also new jobs created – it was about 'seamlessness' – so you actually had a lot of PDs [position descriptions] with the same job description and the same title. If you have a group of ten people with the same customer service roles and tasks, then who is actually accountable for it? So, there was a lot of non-accountability, which made people feel very frustrated. A lot of people left. A lot of people's behaviour and attitude became so disruptive that they had to be asked to leave, but they weren't replaced.

. . . [people] were confused, unsure, they were pushing boundaries and they weren't comfortable and confident in what they were doing. Which is a real shame, and a lot of people left because of that.

(group leader, cultural services, city council, Lonehill)

Not only did the stress of the restructure cause staff attrition (placing added pressure on remaining staff) but team leaders themselves also felt uncomfortable and out of their depth in their new roles.

Across all three case studies, respondents described stressful circumstances that were a direct result of convergence, and that threatened their institution's capability of performing essential functions, such as exhibitions and collection development. As the manager of Westlands explained, the curator, whose previous experience had revolved around the art gallery, lacked confidence in museum work, giving rise to his reluctance to embark on museum exhibitions:

[The curator] has an aim to begin a series of shows in the museum that are going to be called 'Village Town City.' Three separate shows. . . . He is very keen to do it because he's a local boy, so he wants to tell that story. So, I think the desire is there, but it's just a daunting task ahead of him. I think sometimes it stuns and scares him a bit, makes you think, 'I don't know if I'm capable of doing that.'

(manager of Westlands)

At the time the interviews were conducted in 2011, the manager stated that 24 of the 31 exhibitions staged by Westlands in the previous year had been visual arts–based, demonstrating the degree to which the museum component had become less active than the gallery.

Above all, these examples underscore the counterproductive effects of the broadened, cross-domain responsibilities attached to the new roles ushered in through convergence. In many cases, new job descriptions fragmented employees' time to focus on specific tasks, failed to recognise the value of specialist expertise, set up hasty transitions into cross-disciplinary roles and neglected to support staff through constructive professional development and training. According to many participants, these factors, combined with increasing expectations regarding services and program delivery, challenged employees' self-confidence and motivation and therefore the sustainability of the existing organisational structure. Summing up this sentiment, the cultural services group leader at Lonehill stated,

With the cultural precinct we have and the budget we have, why aren't we [achieving] a national profile? Why aren't we being the innovative [centre of] creative excellence we should be? Why aren't we role models? Why aren't we leading the way? . . . I think we're working within a framework that couldn't make anybody be 'the best.'

(group leader, cultural services, city council, Lonehill)

Conclusion: Misdirection, disunity and compelled collaboration

The findings described in this chapter demonstrate a range of outcomes of convergence that are significant to leadership, organisational design, role descriptions and responsibilities and professional cooperation within cultural institutions. However, the fundamental interest behind this book is the extent to which convergence of GLAMs affects interpretive museum practices. How does an analysis of the management and organisational structures of hybrid institutions improve our understanding of this issue?

While the formulation of administrative frameworks for converged institutions mostly occurs at the level of local government cultural services departments and senior managers, these contexts manifest themselves in the everyday professional practices, collaborations and performance of staff. Rather than remaining peripheral to the daily function of individual departments and employees, the research findings indicate that issues such as strategic planning, change management processes, leadership, resource allocation, professional development and the reconfiguration of professional roles are central to the ways in which staff are able to deploy their skills and expertise to enhance both physical and intellectual access to various collections.

Arguably, resistance to change is a common by-product of major restructuring in any organisation, and the expression of related frustrations by interviewees in this research is not unexpected, nor does it necessarily predict negative outcomes for converged collections. However, the information provided by the participants demonstrates that some of the negative results of convergence were more than attitudinal. With regard to museum collections in particular, my analysis reveals that staff in the majority of case studies felt that their fundamental professional obligations in areas such as the preservation, documentation and research of collections, as well as exhibition development and renewal, were significantly compromised through the convergence model.

At the heart of the various dysfunctions of convergence lies ambiguity around institutional purpose. In all three cases presented here, the benefits that organisations were supposed to derive through integration and hybridisation were not clearly articulated to staff members and stakeholder communities. Rather, convergence projects were often motivated by a desire to capitalise on available government funding or reduce local government expenditure. Local councils focussed disproportionately on building iconic facilities and directed spending towards capital works, without the complementary forward planning and provision for ongoing operational funding to support the development of high-quality, locally relevant programs.

Without a strong corporate vision to guide their activities, staff members felt disenfranchised and antagonistic towards the idea of convergence, predisposing them to less collaborative work practices. They developed their own goals and strategies, often with a narrow focus on their particular collection area. Respondents identified the need for leaders of converged institutions to embody and demonstrate the core competencies inherent to the convergence model: cross-disciplinary competence, equal respect for and understanding of different specialisations and openness to collaboration. The absence of these qualities encouraged the (re)formation of isolated professional silos, offsetting the advantages of convergence for communication between staff and collaborative project work.

The potential for professional cross-fertilisation and acquisition of cross-disciplinary expertise was further hampered by the appointment of under-qualified staff into converged collection and management roles, resulting in leadership bias and lack of recognition for specialist expertise. The lack of institutional commitment and frameworks for professional development, together with time limitations experienced by staff, also contributed as barriers to cross-disciplinary training.

Although it is convenient to address each of these management issues independently, doing so comes at the expense of recognising their interconnectedness within the workplace environment and systems that give shape to the converged institutional context for museum collection practices. For example, the absence of a clear, theoretically informed rationale for convergence, together with a non-consultative change management approach, can create the impression that convergence is simply a bureaucratic efficiency model that is externally imposed on an organisation's staff. Likewise, the tendency for local governments to allocate resources to the building of new converged cultural facilities, rather than their ongoing operational requirements, creates a precarious position for collection professionals. Tasked with fulfilling government and public expectations for increased numbers of exhibitions, public programs and services while juggling restricted staffing and budgets, staff members are placed under pressure. In response, they may retreat to their established areas of expertise and work patterns, diminishing the possibility for meaningful engagement and collaboration across professional fields.

Significantly, this research challenges the feasibility of some of the basic assumptions about convergence. For example, respondents across the case studies viewed the prospect of gaining genuine cross-disciplinary expertise with scepticism, observing that staff retained a bias in favour of their original area of specialisation, regardless of (and sometimes in active opposition to) revised job descriptions. When silos of professional practice persist, the promise of convergence enabling the integrated use of diverse cultural collections, or highlighting the connections between different forms of cultural expression, is unlikely to be fully realised.

Speaking metaphorically, one respondent underscored the nascency of convergence as a model, comparing it to the monster created by Dr Frankenstein that, once brought to life, is abandoned to find its own meaning and viability under sometimes adverse circumstances:

> So much sorrow and pain for that monster who gets created, almost through a flawed concept . . . I look forward to seeing convergence 4.0 because it will probably be getting closer to being a practical thing. By then, people will be used to working across a number of institutions and be able to maintain enough specialist experience to make that a worthy place. . . . We've given birth to this monster. Now how do we control it, how do we get it to do what we want it to do, how do we stop it from hurting people?
>
> (collections and exhibitions officer, Lonehill)

My analysis of the operational dysfunctions of GLAM convergence indicates that problems at the level of interpretive practice (Chapter 3) are, in fact, prefigured by leadership and management frameworks that dictate the parameters of everyday collection work and the kinds of interactions that take place between specialist staff and disciplinary practices. Reductive bureaucratic motivations for convergence that fail to adequately consider differences in how different types of collections are documented, researched, interpreted and used can produce hybridity that is only skin deep. A lack of functionality and harmony between the resulting institution's constituent parts can threaten its meaningfulness and viability. In the following chapter, I focus on the question of sustainability by synthesising the theoretical position of the book with the case study findings, evaluating whether GLAM convergence represents an opportunity or impediment to the interpretative vibrancy of museums.

Notes

1 For a description of the advantages of a 'practice theory' approach to museum research, see Conal McCarthy's introduction to the *Museum Practice* volume of the *International Handbooks of Museum Studies*, 2015 (xlv–xlvi).
2 Description of the rationale for convergence by the group leader, cultural services, city council, Lonehill.
3 For a discussion of the continuing trend in government financial support for capital works over operational funding in the cultural sector, see Robinson 2018.
4 From interview with the CEO, district council, Maunga Tapu.
5 The cultural development manager at Lonehill made similar observations, stating that competent staff members were compelled to compensate for those who were less effective in their roles.

Conclusion
Interpretive sustainability in the hybrid institution

> *To have an excellent integrated service, we needed to have excellent component parts, in terms of our professional knowledge and skills. . . . The parts have to be excellent, and if the whole is greater than the sum of its parts, you would expect it to be fabulous.*
>
> —former manager of Maunga Tapu

Under-researched and conceptually oversimplified, the growing prevalence of structurally converged collecting institutions has outstripped efforts to understand the impacts of hybridisation on the fundamental processes of meaning-making native to each domain of practice. The rapidly expanding notion of convergence has already moved beyond the arguably closed system of libraries, museums, galleries and archives. Future forecasters now enthusiastically anticipate hybridisation of collecting institutions with a much wider range of public service providers in the hope of addressing a swathe of community needs in response to an ever-decreasing funding environment. Not only do these new demands challenge the conventional remit and expertise of collecting institutions but they also underplay the role of these organisations – and museums in particular – in interpreting and providing access to the cultural heritage significance of their collections. From the pages of *Museum 2040* (2017), it is unclear whether the paintings and objects that populate exhibition spaces hybridised with well-being and cognitive health centres (7), schools (17) and community centres hosting meditation classes (19) act as little more than window dressing for what are otherwise multipurpose service hubs. What justifies retention and investment in specialised museum interpretive practices in the light of other pressing social needs, especially when resources are scarce?

Interpretive sustainability 97

With a focus on museums, the intention of this book has been to trouble the easy conflation of 'GLAM' around generic notions of community service. By distilling and reasserting the value of museum practices for knowledge creation around cultural objects, I suggest that the layered processes of meaning-making endemic to museums are crucial in scaffolding diverse and satisfying engagements with the materials in their care. These processes, I argue, are key to fulfilling museums' responsibilities to their communities by sparking generative dialogue about issues relating to historical awareness, individual and collective identities, place and politics.

In this final chapter, I provide a synthesis of the issues raised throughout the book in the context of the need to preserve interpretive practice in museums, introducing the idea of *interpretive sustainability* as a new criterion within the broader rubric of sustainability. I propose ways in which converged institutions can maintain and enhance this function to ensure the ongoing relevance and genuine democratisation of cultural collections. The concept of interpretive sustainability can and, I argue, should be a strategic concern in determining the feasibility of future organisational restructures in which the blurring of domain boundaries, or even the hybridisation of collecting institutions with non–collections-focussed organisations, is being considered.

An evidence-based critique of the conventional wisdoms of the convergence debate

The well-rehearsed yet reductive argument that distinctive museum, library and archival practices merely perpetuate an arbitrary historical division of the domains has served to trivialise important disciplinary distinctions in the ways in which collections are researched, organised, documented and made accessible through different kinds of repositories. As discussed in Chapter 1 of this book, the perceived 'silos' of domain-based collection practice have been thrown in sharp relief against the advent of increasingly sophisticated online database tools that promote interoperability, prompting efforts to produce a common language for describing data about diverse collections and spurring initiatives to unite collection information in a borderless digital environment. The compelling ideal of universal digital access to cultural collections-repositioned as multipurpose economic and social resources with new utility to a broad spectrum of public, private and government stakeholders-dovetails neatly with cultural policy shifts around the world that emphasise the instrumental benefits of cultural provision.

The same motivations underpin moves to integrate and hybridise brick-and-mortar collecting and cultural institutions. At all levels of government, the promise of operational efficiencies, improved accessibility and higher return on taxpayer investment has motivated the establishment of converged collecting institutions. At least ideally, domain boundaries dissolve and multifunctional, agile staff structures promote disciplinary cross-fertilisation and creative use of all collection resources around the shared purpose of maximised public benefit. Perhaps blinded by the tantalising possibility that convergence could deliver reductions in ongoing funding requirements while simultaneously producing institutions that activate the full knowledge potential of cultural collections, agitations towards domain integration have tended to gloss over the practicalities of achieving genuine convergence. In response, the core motivation of this book has been to reinsert a more thorough investigation of meaning-making processes into a now conventional discourse around convergence that circumvents detailed considerations of professional practice, preferring instead a fast-forward (or mechanistic quick fix) approach to its predicted positive outcomes.

Investigating three cases of convergence using a theoretical framework based on museological analysis of interpretation and knowledge creation around collections, I have sought to understand how hybrid institutional environments are organised, how they function, the degree of crossdisciplinary collaboration among staff and the extent to which the interpretive potential of collections is actualised in these settings. Acknowledging a range of potential research directions, I chose to focus on a qualitative methodology that would highlight ground-level, 'insider' perspectives of daily collection, providing a window onto development and delivery of collection-based public programs and sharing of disciplinary expertise.

While further study is undoubtedly warranted, the research presented in these pages complicates and challenges the fundamental assumption that convergence produces what are termed 'knowledge institutions,' or that the integration of collecting organisations automatically creates improved potential for knowledge creation.

Convergence in practice

Museum professionals are in the business of crafting encounters with collection information for users and visitors, rather than disseminating knowledge. As a 'species of information retrieval system' (Buckland 1991, 359), museums rely on an interconnected framework of processes for accumulating and organising information around collections. These processes – such as development of collection policies, object description and cataloguing,

Interpretive sustainability 99

research, conservation, narrative construction, exhibition design and public program development – and the staff who perform them orchestrate the ways in which visitors and other collection users engage with information in museum contexts. If we accept this as the mechanism through which 'knowledge' is produced in museums – i.e. as a dialogic process involving the museum producers of information and the users who interact with it – then the onus falls on the capacity of museum staff to carry out the activities that produce information, and information encounters, around museum collections. The key themes that have emerged through the research presented here attest to both gains and losses to the 'knowledge potential' of collections through hybridised institutional models.

Keeping the promise: moving beyond the efficiency paradigm

Based on the accounts provided by participants in this research, collection professionals recognise the rich potential for convergence to unite typologically and descriptively diverse collection materials, creating the possibility for all kinds of artefacts and documents to be cross-referenced and juxtaposed to produce new, enriched understandings of culture and its development. Ideally, convergence can act as a catalyst for dynamic exchanges of collection information, facilitating meaningful connections between different modes of collection description and activating new interpretive horizons.

By taking advantage of the scope for integrated programming across thematically related collections, the potential exists for hybrid institutions to contribute to deeper and more holistic exploration of local histories and cultures, exposing the interdependency between diverse objects (i.e. artefacts, artworks, documents, images, literature, etc.) and allowing thematic relationships between different cultural forms to be made explicit.

From the standpoint of the interpretive practices that construct collection information in the museum context, a strategic commitment to this culturally integrative model of convergence would certainly influence the adoption of cross-disciplinary collaboration and sharing of expertise, to which many proponents of convergence aspire. In an ideal situation, organisational leadership, the design of staff structures, recruitment and day-to-day professional practices would align around mutual respect across disciplinary boundaries, manifested also by the fair division of financial resources, recognition of the value of specialist expertise and institution-wide dedication to collection research, preservation and provision of collection access, as well as delivery of diverse public programs across all domains. Acknowledgement of the role of professional museum practice in framing unique contexts for understanding collection objects would be retained while simultaneously encouraging museum specialists to collaborate with other collection professionals, allowing for the emergence of poignant, innovative interpretations of collection content. In these ways, convergence would facilitate the production of collection information and provide scaffolding for user interactions with objects and information resources. Converged institutions would be more than the sum of the individual organisations that had been brought together in their formation, creating a new collaborative, relational context for interpreting and engaging with cultural material.

Indeed, the case studies outlined in this book do provide evidence of the positive potential for staff to coordinate their activities and prioritise higher levels of collaboration in pursuit of integrated cultural experiences. At Lonehill and Maunga Tapu, convergence brought together, and allowed for joint management of, museum (largely social history) and local studies collections with the purpose of maintaining and responding to the heritage of their respective geographical regions. By contrast, at Westlands, the experience of separating the museum and local studies collections caused significant impediments to preservation, research and public access to thematically related material, proving – by virtue of its absence – that integration of these collection types makes good sense for local cultural organisations.

The creation of both formal and informal communication frameworks through convergence also translated into tangible benefits for the documentation and interpretation of museum collections. Many respondents across all the case studies agreed that greater communication between staff created potential for collections to be used more creatively, leading to the exploration of alternative readings of collection significance and a collaborative approach to the development of exhibitions, publications and other public programs.

Respondents across the case studies also acknowledged that convergence was accompanied by the relocation of facilities into new buildings designed and constructed to house the various collections. Renewal of infrastructure was important not only for increasing the public profile of institutions but also for providing better facilities for collection storage and conservation, as well as new exhibition spaces. Although not intrinsically linked to the concept of convergence, the promised operational efficiencies of the model were leveraged to persuade state and local authorities of the long-term benefit of capital investment. The new amenities contributed to physical collection environments more conducive to collection care, research and presentation.

In terms of sustainability, it is also important to remember that any discussion of the creation and provision of museum collection information becomes purely academic if a museum ceases to exist. The incorporation

Interpretive sustainability 101

of formerly historical society collections into local government administrations (Westlands, Lonehill), together with the subsequent formalisation and professionalisation of museum services (Maunga Tapu), enabled improvements in interpretive practices simply by virtue of guaranteeing the ongoing existence of those collections.

In summary, the restructuring of organisational structures, staff communication and collaborative frameworks – and improvements to physical infrastructure that accompanied the adoption of a converged institutional model at the institutions covered by this research – substantiates the potential of convergence to broaden and deepen cultural engagement. By bringing together typologically diverse but thematically related collections while simultaneously creating opportunities for staff from different disciplinary backgrounds to cooperate across domain boundaries, convergence can reshape the operational parameters of collecting institutions and offer new possibilities for the innovative use of collection information. In the ideal scenario, the beneficiaries of these changes are public users for whom convergence enables easier access to different kinds of collections and the information resources surrounding them, as well as the production of unique and compelling programs that interpret collections in terms of local significance. However, drawing on the accounts of respondents in the case studies examined for this research, is convergence able to consistently deliver on the promise of improved access and engagement with cultural collections?

If one were to judge the success of convergence purely according to the general benefits articulated above, it would be difficult not to conclude that convergence achieves its principal goals. That is, as an integrative model for the provision of cultural collections, convergence realises the aim of uniting the different products of human society and culture, enabling those forms to interact to produce enriched understanding within each field of collection practice, as well as enabling objects to be interpreted from a variety of disciplinary viewpoints.

In reality, however, this research shows that the ideals of convergence are seldom realised to their full potential. Not only does the leadership of converged institutions rarely embody or articulate this vision of convergence with sufficient clarity but work practices in different collection areas also reflect a lack of joint purpose. Many of the changes brought about by convergence – such as organisational restructuring, cross-disciplinary role descriptions, perceived leadership bias and high expectations regarding the turnaround of exhibitions – actively work against the realisation of comprehensive engagement by staff with museum collections and productive dialogue between collection areas.

Contrary to the ubiquitous 'knowledge institution' envisaged by the proponents of convergence, the case study research shows that employees perceive GLAM integration as an overwhelmingly efficiency-driven economic model with only loosely expressed conceptual objectives. Institutions' failure to clearly articulate a unified purpose had a cascading effect on downstream planning and decision-making around change management, organisational restructuring, budget allocation and public programming objectives (the desired balance between in-house versus touring exhibitions on offer and so on). At Maunga Tapu in particular, the absence of a clear, unified institutional vision reinforced insular work practices (disciplinary 'silos'), heightened competition for financial resources and stymied cross-domain teamwork.

The case studies show that emphasis on cost minimisation dominated restructuring processes, limiting the ability of staff to consistently deliver innovative and engaging programs derived from collection research and interpretation. To varying extents, the persistence of insular practices at all the case study sites was exacerbated by what respondents perceived as disciplinary prejudice on the part of institutional managers, who often appeared to privilege programs, interpretations of content and departments in the organisation that reflected their own original area of specialisation. In other words, none had leaders who embodied and modelled the cross-disciplinary ideal of convergence.

At Westlands and Lonehill, convergence restructuring penetrated down to the design of individual position descriptions, where roles focussing on designated collection areas were repurposed to encompass the entire scope of collection holdings.[1] Likewise, staff members trained in specific disciplines – such as librarianship, archives management, museum collection management and curatorship – were redeployed into these newly devised roles and expected to function competently across all areas.

Rather than engendering professional growth and genuine cross-disciplinarity, staff employed in converged roles encountered a compounding series of difficulties that prevented them from engaging equally, and productively, with each collection within their area of responsibility. An important underlying factor at both Westlands and Lonehill was the mismatched recruitment of staff into roles for which they lacked training and experience, coupled with inconsistent (and often retrospectively implemented) strategies for professional development. At Lonehill, generalist role descriptions had the effect of scattering employees' attention and responsibilities across too many areas simultaneously, reducing accountability and productivity in any single area. The result of staff working in roles for which they were under-qualified or inexperienced was what one respondent at Westlands described as 'process conflict': a sense of uncertainty produced through the necessity of navigating asymmetric disciplinary knowledges, collection management techniques, interpretive frameworks and project-specific workflows.

These difficulties became intensified by unrealistically high expectations of productivity owing to the management focus on operational efficiency. Respondents in all case studies perceived their organisations to be understaffed, creating an environment where overburdened employees lacked the time necessary to develop competencies in other collection areas.

In such situations, the risk is not only that museum-based activities – especially those that contribute to collection documentation and construction of thematic linkages between objects – may be given lower priority in comparison to activities more familiar to staff trained in another discipline but also that staff not experienced in museum work may, in fact, be blind to these processes simply because they do not know why they are significant, or perhaps that they even exist.

For museum collections and the production of information about them, these limitations have considerable impact. Combined with the self-doubt experienced by some staff working outside their area of expertise (Westlands, Lonehill), a number of non–museum-trained respondents described their reluctance to embark on museum collection research, revisions to permanent exhibition spaces and development of travelling exhibitions using the in-house collections. In effect, the interpretive potential of collections was not being explored because of the organisational structure and management priorities brought about by convergence.

Converged collections: more meaningful or mute?

In all three case studies, respondents pointed to condensed timeframes for research-intensive tasks such as collection development and significance assessment as factors that compromised the eventual narrative flow of exhibitions, as well as diminishing the capacity for display areas to be updated. While these shortcomings could, arguably, be attributed to the pressure accompanying the opening of any new facility, subsequent staffing and resourcing issues directly related to convergence clearly proved influential in constraining the ability of museum collection staff to make necessary adjustments to permanent exhibitions.

In the context of knowledge production – that is, providing scaffolded opportunities for users to interact with collection information – respondents in all the case studies reported feeling limited in their ability to conduct original or extended research of collections, improve collection documentation or produce innovative exhibitions and programs. For example, the manager at Westlands criticised the permanent exhibition's failure to engage with the history of European settlement in the region and the resulting conflicts and displacement of local Indigenous populations, which continued to have a lasting impact on community relations and social issues in the area. Combined with the fixed design of the permanent exhibition area, the curator at Westlands also expressed frustration at his limited capacity to reconceptualise the permanent exhibitions. The pressures accompanying the curator's combined duties across museum and gallery operations, as well as his training exclusively in visual arts, represented constant impediments to the effectiveness of his work. With the same constraints limiting the development of temporary exhibitions, local Aboriginal and contact history remained an under-interpreted theme within the institution, implicitly alienating a significant segment of the local population and rendering these aspects of the region's history invisible to tourists and local community members alike.

In the context of changing exhibitions, respondents in all case studies expressed concern at the prioritisation of temporary exhibition programs, which favoured imported travelling displays over exhibitions developed in-house. Most remarkable was the admission made by one respondent at Maunga Tapu that his organisation originally had no budget allocation whatsoever for the development of temporary exhibitions. Respondents at Lonehill noted that the predominance of hosted touring exhibitions reduced the organisation's ability to explore the cultural uniqueness of the local area. It also reduced the attention to behind-the-scenes activities, such as cataloguing and research of the in-house collections, as staff scrambled to keep up with the demands of a busy exhibitions and events calendar. In effect, collections remained in stasis – warehoused – as pre-packaged touring 'product' was 'churned in and out.'

Based on these outcomes, the efficacy of convergence is questionable when it comes to demonstrating appreciable benefits for the production of meaning around museum collections. Likewise, convergence becomes problematic when considering the goal of state and local governments to increase accessibility to arts and culture, acknowledging cultural diversity and facilitating the representation and participation of all population segments in cultural programs.

By shaping the institutional environment for collection work, strategic planning, management frameworks, leadership, reporting structures and other institutional frameworks come into focus as strong determinants of interpretive practice. The ability of 'street-level' staff to productively interact with collections may become limited by circumstantial constraints, including understaffing, insufficient budget allocation towards collection research and exhibition development, the absence of clear institutional goals or a poorly devised organisational structure that reduces staff productivity. Alternatively, difficulties stem from insufficient staff expertise in converged role descriptions. Employees may lack the necessary training, time, confidence or authority to adequately research, document and perform

Interpretive sustainability 105

activities related to extended collection interpretation in the form of exhibition narrative production or writing exhibition texts and other museum publications, designing user engagements with objects and displays and so on. Importantly, the underutilisation of in-house collections, both for rotation of objects in permanent exhibition areas and for the creation of locally specific temporary displays, restricts the ability of institutions to explore and communicate important narratives about a particular area's history or the relationships between its constituent social and cultural groups.

Constraints on staff engagement with collections have the potential to affect the creation of information at all stages of a museum object's life cycle, from initial classification, provenance gathering and documentation at the point of acquisition, creation and maintenance of object files and electronic databases to significance assessment, project-based thematic research and the development of exhibitions. Each of these activities produces tangible information artefacts that constitute a complementary and equally significant 'collection' alongside objects themselves (Matassa 2011). Each of these information resources represents a potential point of access for collection users. And so any reduction in the availability or quality of collection information equates to a reduction in the scope and meaningfulness of user interactions with objects, with direct implications for their 'knowledge' value.

Interpretation and sustainability

Cultural meanings that develop around collections are 'situated and contextual' (Macdonald 2006, 2) – that is, the meaning of objects is not innate, fixed or preordained, but rather evolves in direct relation to the performance of museum processes within specific organisational settings. As such, meaning is tied to the aptitude and skills of curators and other collection professionals, the employment of particular methodologies for building the informational record around collection objects (i.e. classification, research, interpretation of social, historical, artistic and other forms of significance, etc.) and the aims, disciplinary bent, resources and policy frameworks of the institution. Objects are fundamentally 'multivocal' (Annis 1994, 21); individual institutions provide the particular contexts within which the array of potential significations of objects is filtered and then amplified through tangible information resources.

From this perspective, practices associated with collection documentation, research and public presentation come into focus as fundamental to the ways in which the information end products surrounding collections actually take shape. At this level, differences between libraries, archives, museums and galleries are less about the typological distinctions between the material collected by each domain and more about discipline-based approaches to the provision of collection access, as well as practices for identifying, organising and communicating collection value. Here, the maintenance of disciplinary differences becomes important in preserving multiple interpretive contexts for understanding collection items. It is in this context that the notion of 'interpretive sustainability' of a collection, rather than merely its management or financial sustainability, comes to the fore.

Conversely, in situations where professional, domain-specific practices are thwarted or break down – for example, through the recruitment of underqualified staff into cross-disciplinary collection roles, the absence of clear institutional goals, organisational structures that inhibit collaboration or the simple lack of funding or time for basic cataloguing and research of collections – the potential of collections to acquire meaning is also curtailed.

In my earlier critique of the labelling of converged collecting organisations as 'knowledge institutions' (Chapter 2), I referred to the differences between information and knowledge, but also the dependency of the latter on the former (Buckland 1991; Hislop 2002; Stehr and Ufer 2009; Jones 2010). The risk of convergence is that, if collection professionals are prevented from interacting with objects to produce various forms of information, those objects cannot become accessible to end users for processes of knowledge creation. Without appropriate levels of interpretation and contextualisation, the mere existence and preservation of objects – whether co-located or not with other collections – become effectively moot.

Paradoxically, this eventuality contradicts the ideals of inclusion and cultural democracy that have underpinned shifts in cultural policy (and funding) towards local government administration of community arts, cultural facilities and programs from the early 1980s and which form the backdrop to the adoption of convergence in the case studies presented here. How can the communities feel genuinely represented by, and invested in, collections if active and innovative interpretation of those collections is not allowed to occur?

Activating the unfulfilled potential of convergence

The case studies show that convergence undoubtedly sets up the potential for changes to work practices that can lead to enriched engagement with museum collections and their significant meanings. The co-location of exhibition areas, establishment of frameworks for official and informal communication between staff across disciplinary boundaries and improved physical infrastructure for the preservation and presentation of collections, as well as ease of access for visitors and users, puts in place important prerequisites for convergence to trigger vibrant interplay between collection areas that could result in new insights and forms of engagement with community heritage, local histories and creative expression.

However, my case studies also demonstrate that the implementation of converged organisational models can simultaneously sabotage the ability of staff to realise this potential by creating impediments to the performance of museum practices that are essential to building comprehensive information frameworks around collections. The absence of a conceptual vision can give way to mechanistic convergences that fail to articulate the cultural value of collections and relegate labour-intensive specialist collection tasks to secondary importance.

Fundamental aspects of museum work, such as accessioning and provenance research, study of collections independent of immediate programming deadlines, compilation of comprehensive documentation and maintenance of databases and finding aids, all come under threat with these changes. Likewise, the work of library, archives and gallery professionals can be impacted, not only placing constraints on the expertise and practices within specific collecting areas but also limiting the potential for intellectual linkages to be made across domain boundaries. Taking these learnings into account, what would a more effective, genuinely hybridised and 'interpretively sustainable' converged institution look like?

Rethinking performance indicators in a decreasing funding environment

In 2006, prominent museologist Hugh Genoways warned that museums, which had historically apportioned relatively equal resources to their four core areas (collections, documentation, preservation and interpretation), were under pressure from funding bodies to deliver marketable programs and increase their public interface, sometimes at the expense of care, maintenance and scholarly research of collections (Genoways 2006, 225–26). Similarly, in the early 2000s, Hedstrom and King acknowledged that financial pressures had forced many cultural institutions, especially museums, to become increasingly market-orientated at the risk of producing 'exhibitions that are popular and trendy rather than critical and thought-provoking' (Hedstrom and King 2004, 22). My case studies demonstrate a similar trade-off when collection work competes with the preparation of outward-facing public programs for staff time. In all the case studies presented here, a high turnaround of travelling exhibitions resulted in deferred research and interpretation of in-house collections as staff scrambled to meet rolling deadlines imposed by a constant turnover of temporary displays. Especially when housed in newly built facilities, converged institutions were under pressure to maintain a dynamic calendar of public events, which was seen as visible proof of value for money and therefore a justification of the convergence model. In this environment, exploration of local cultural heritage can be threatened by a protracted hiatus in the development and interpretation of in-house collections.

As long as public funding allocations to the collections sector continue to decline, it is unlikely that the prime motivation for the establishment of converged collecting and cultural institutions – the promise of financial efficiency – will diminish. In recognising a degree of inevitability to this ongoing trend, it is nevertheless possible to envisage an alternative form of hybridisation in which interpretive sustainability becomes central to the planning and operations of new institutions.

In the context of convergence, recognition of the importance of collection interpretation calls on funding bodies (state and local governments in particular) to recalibrate performance indicators, with less emphasis on superficial turnover of exhibitions and other events and programs as markers of productivity. In consultation with street-level collection workers and management staff, governments could develop policies and incentives that reward collection care and research, such as progressively increasing levels of ongoing operational funding that can be unlocked through attainment of best practice standards in collection care, research and public programs developed from local content.

Genuinely converged vision, leadership and organisational structure

My research demonstrates that conceptually vague or mechanistic visions for converged institutions sabotage the potential for genuine collaboration across GLAM specialisation. Without clearly defined objectives around the benefits of combining museum, library, archive and gallery functions, individual operational areas fall into unhealthy competition for visibility (and resources) within the institution, filling the strategic vacuum with self-formulated priorities that can pull the institution's operations in contradictory directions, as well as engendering mistrust between divisions.

Recent research within the rubric of 'practice theory' (McCarthy 2015) is highlighting the importance of leadership, management structures and communication flows in the capacity for collecting institutions to remain dynamic, cohesive and responsive to emerging challenges. For example, in case study research methodologically analogous to my own, Yuha Jung has examined the workplace culture of a Midwestern art museum in the United States, finding that poorly defined organisational objectives combined with a top-down management system work to undermine collaborative work practices, eroding the ability of staff to adapt to new challenges and therefore the organisation's resilience, flexibility and growth (Jung 2016, 170–71). In particular, Jung observes that staff cooperation becomes fractured and a 'compartmentalized and patchwork culture' prevails in the absence of a clear vision for the museum – a situation further compounded by a hierarchical management approach that disregards the value of staff members' disciplinary knowledge and expertise (172). How much more acute, then, is the challenge of creating a collaborative and adaptive culture in converged institutions that attempts to combine not only different collections but also the associated domain-specific practices that go with them?

To avoid a fractured working environment, converged institutions require objectives that are resolved at the conceptual, rather than merely operational, level. Strategic planning, management priorities, organisational design and collaborative frameworks should be rooted in institutional visions that authentically engage with what convergence ideally means for knowledge creation. Measures can then be put in place to ensure that the constituent parts of a converged organisation can not only coexist within a single management structure but can also be meaningfully hybridised to produce innovative interpretations of collections with flow-on benefits in differentiating the unique cultural value of collections and creating locally relevant content.

A special responsibility lies with managers of converged collecting institutions to uphold a unified vision and understand how various operational functions and activities contribute to its realisation. Unavoidably, this necessitates literacy in the professional practices of all the collecting domains as well as differences in the provision of access to collections. Among the case studies presented here, none had leaders who embodied and modelled the cross-disciplinary ideal of convergence. As discussed below, training is needed to ensure that institutional leaders remain sensitive to the synergies (and differences) between the disciplines and navigate a procedurally and conceptually viable path to greater integration.[2]

Professional training for hybrid GLAMs

An important underlying factor at the case study institutions was the mismatched recruitment of staff into roles for which they lacked training and experience, coupled with inconsistent (and often retrospectively implemented) strategies for professional development. The creation of cross-domain roles resulted in what one respondent at Westlands described as 'process conflict,' with staff unable to effectively manage competing demands around collection documentation, workflows and public programs development. According to the research respondents, the difficulties associated with genuine cross-disciplinarity extended to top-tier managers, whose professional qualifications and expertise in a single domain of collection practice influenced the prioritisation of particular operational divisions and functions.

It remains to be seen whether the acquisition of authentically nonpartisan, comprehensive cross-domain collection expertise is possible. Nevertheless, concerns about the feasibility of informed professional practice across collecting domains point, at the very least, to the requirement for new approaches to the training of GLAM professionals.

While numerous commentaries have suggested that collaboration and convergence will lead to the acquisition of cross-domain knowledge between library, archive and museum staff, leading to the cross-fertilisation of ideas, innovation and development across the sectors (Dempsey 2000; Miller 2000; Clement 2007; Zorich, Waibel and Erway 2008; Boaden and Clement 2009; Stapleton 2007; Duff et al. 2013), corresponding curriculum changes have been slow to take shape.

In 2009, Canadian museum informatics researcher and consultant Jennifer Trant observed that tertiary curricula for the training of museum professionals, librarians and archivists continued to promote traditional differences between the domains in spite of policy and institutional shifts towards collaboration and cross-domain convergence (Trant 2009; see also similar observations in Given and McTavish 2010; Tanackovic and Badurina 2009). In 2013, Canadian researchers noted that the skill set required for effective research and interdisciplinary collection work across domains would require a 'new breed of information professional' (Duff et al. 2013), noting that the emergence of Canadian iSchools (library and information science education focussing on technologically mediated information management) was one development supporting cross-domain professional education. While significant within the parameters of digital convergence, such archive- and library science–driven initiatives arguably represent a much more limited contribution to the training of staff for work in physically integrated institutions.

In 2016, the United States–based OCLC (Online Computer Library Centre) released its 'National Agenda for Continuing Education and Professional Development across Libraries, Archives, and Museums,' a strategic plan to better align continuing education and professional development in the collections sector. Drawing on three years of consultation carried out by the Coalition to Advance Learning in Archives, Libraries and Museums,[3] the Agenda underscores the common challenges faced by museum, library and archive professionals in responding to escalating technological change, demands for greater efficiency and an increasing array of community service obligations (2016, 5). The plan formulates four overarching goals to reinforce the GLAM sector through coordinated upskilling measures. The range of associated strategies emphasises the need to identify synergies in practice and common continuing education needs, establish formal cross-domain professional networks, advocate for the need to resource professional learning and develop joint curricula for continuing education. However, in the context of interpretive sustainability, a review of the Agenda's plan raises a number of unresolved issues. First, because it is targeted at continuing education rather than the structure of foundational tertiary qualifications for museum, library and archive professionals, such a plan could be seen as little more than a Band-Aid response to the practical needs of workers in converged institutions, where professionals are already operating in an environment where disciplinary boundaries and responsibilities have blurred. Second, by focussing on commonalities in service delivery across libraries, archives and museums, the report fails to address the question of how specialised back-of-house practices – particularly in terms of research and interpretation of collections – can be sustained and potentially shared.

So, it seems, the training of GLAM professionals at both undergraduate and postgraduate levels has so far maintained its traditional emphasis on single domains of practice, lagging behind the trend for integration and hybridisation of both digital and brick-and-mortar institutions. In 2018, the University of Toronto's Faculty of Information, which also hosts a master of museum studies program, launched a new postgraduate unit of study dedicated to exploring the intersections and tension between library, archive and museum theory and practice. While no comprehensive inventory of existing undergraduate and postgraduate programs in these fields has been conducted, it seems that this unit is one of the first attempts at integrating professional training at the formal level. Until consolidated effort is invested in devising new forms of cross-domain training, converged institutions will continue to be established, managed and staffed by individuals who, perhaps, embrace the ideals of cross-disciplinary work practices but lack the theoretical frameworks and practical skills to sidestep the trial and error processes of 'learning on the job.'

Conclusion: realising the value of interpretive sustainability

In Chapter 1, I quoted Stephen Weil, who, channelling the democratising ethos and public service orientation of the 'new museology,' wrote that the museum had become

> a transformed and redirected institution that can . . . use its very special competencies in dealing with objects to contribute positively to the quality of individual human lives and to enhance the well-being of human communities.
>
> (Weil 1999, 231)

Within this ideal, museum collections and the 'very special competencies' of museum professionals – their knowledge of collections and interpretive capacities – enable meaningful interactions with collections that invigorate and deepen cultural engagement, producing the sought-after social benefits emphasised in policy rhetoric. Implicitly, Weil was underscoring the value of intellectual access to collections and associated collection information, facilitated through interpretive collection practice, as the foundation of museum education and compelling museum experiences.

Within this context, interpretive sustainability is the basic premise and enabler of free exchange of ideas in a museum. It could be defined as the protection of the capacity to re-evaluate and renegotiate accepted histories and identity narratives that are woven around the products of human culture. Interpretive sustainability is about the museum as a site of autonomous, creative and generative dialogue arising through the understanding of collections. As *process* rather than outcome, such exchange only exists if it can be performed – if the museum environment allows for the regeneration of meanings around objects and if those meanings can be given tangible form as exhibitions or public programs. Once articulated, meanings can be evaluated, critiqued and offered as the starting point for ongoing conversations concerning their validity. Ideally, these interpreted meanings serve as utterances within the public sphere that are open to iterative public assessment and contestation, feeding the desire to understand the present through conscious consideration of the human condition across time, culture and place.

In these ways, interpretive sustainability is a precondition to cultural vitality. The maintenance of interpretive dialogue around objects supports the museum as a site of genuine exchange of ideas and cultural values. An interpretively alive museum holds itself suspended in the space where ideas can be expressed, considered, developed and even respectfully rejected. However, any conversation must start somewhere, and for museums, that place is most often the collected object. It is my argument that the distinctive interpretive treatment of collections in museums is central to broader social processes of cultural meaning-making, distinguishing museums from other kinds of collecting institutions. If museums do not exercise this interpretive duty, they risk forfeiting their social relevance, not to mention undermining the rationale for keeping collections at all.

So, the ability to 'act on' collections meaningfully (i.e. producing meaning) needs to be retained if museums are restructured and combined with other collecting institutions; all the more so if they are to be fused with a broader swathe of public services. The museum as cultural forum, activated through practices of interpretation, realises its institutional identity precisely through the capacity to actualise interpretative processes. It is defined through what it *does*, rather than through that of which it is tangibly comprised (its collections, its building). If we accept this definition, then the administrative structure of a museum can certainly be reformulated, but not at the expense of interpretive practice.

In a hybrid environment, collecting institutions ought to be able to broaden their focus, enabling them to incorporate a multitude of thematic relationships between objects (within and across collection boundaries) and create diverse forms of access to collections for the communities that produced them. The potential of convergence lies in sharpening the contours of our understanding of cultural objects, magnifying granular details of the provenance, history and significance of artefacts, as well as allowing us to distinguish subtle differences between collections. The case studies presented in this book demonstrate, however, that convergence can also create near-sightedness, condemning collection workers to see only what is closest to hand, forcing them to work at a superficial level with objects they already know, while sentencing the remaining content of collections to remain hidden and mute in collection stores.

If interpretive sustainability is undercut – either conceptually through the dissolution of interpretive expertise and rigour or by virtue of simply being crowded out of feasible practice by a host of competing 'performance indicators' and output demands – then a museum effectively ceases to exist. Once disqualified as a site of active interpretation of cultural materials, what takes the place of the museum is, for all intents and purposes, a hollow venue with an adjunct warehouse of objects.

Surely, cultural organisations and governments should consider the value of museums, libraries and archives as institutional settings for interpretation – not merely for the informational utility of the individual objects and associated documentation that make up their collections or the cost efficiencies to be gained by combining facilities. By engaging in a discussion about the production of knowledge and meaning around cultural collections, scholars, collection professionals and policy-makers can build a deeper understanding of both the range of significances that can pertain to a single collection item and the role of institutional context in shaping collection information, thereby developing a theoretical rationale for practical decision-making around convergence. With this awareness, those with the capacity to influence convergence projects may indeed be able to identify and develop whatever opportunities are offered by the model for enhanced knowledge creation for end users, and perhaps a more critically and conceptually informed model for convergence can begin to take shape. Without it, we cannot take for granted that the extensive resources invested in achieving convergence will deliver promised improvements in knowledge acquisition and intellectual access to cultural heritage.

114 *Interpretive sustainability*

Notes

1 The original converged organisational structure at Lonehill was revised several times and had substantially reverted to operating around singular collection areas at the time of this research.
2 Australian research (Dunphy 2010; Mulligan and Smith 2010; LGNSW 2017) has shown that the relatively recent development of cultural services divisions within municipal government has resulted in inconsistent approaches to the governance of locally funded cultural organisations. Hence, the expectation of cross-disciplinary competence should also be extended to local and state government arts and culture officers involved in decision-making for the GLAM sector.
3 For a detailed report on the research project that informed the drafting of the Agenda, see Clareson 2016.

Appendix 1
Case study descriptions

Westlands Museum, Gallery and Arts Centre

Westlands is a small organisation of seven full-time equivalent staff[1] located in a regional area of NSW and funded through the local city council. Council statistics show that the city's population is approximately 40,000, with a median age of 36. With a diverse community, over 10% of the city's residents identify as Indigenous. Opened in 2006, Westlands is a convergence of a local social history museum, regional art gallery and community arts centre.

In 1997, the city council assumed responsibility for the museum, which had been administered by the local historical society since the 1950s, with a collection loosely focussed on the history and identity of the people of the region. The regional gallery collection originated through the council in the late 1980s. Around the year 2000, it became apparent that the preservation and storage conditions for the museum were inadequate. At about the same time, it became necessary to relocate the gallery. It was at this time that the plan to develop a joint facility evolved. Recognising that the target audiences and educational objectives for the museum, gallery and proposed community arts centre overlapped, the council resolved to create an integrated facility to house all three functions.

The resulting institution produced a staff structure that was fully 'converged' from the outset, with the key roles of manager, curator, collections officer, education officer and centre coordinator each working across all three facets of the institution. At the time the interviews for this research were conducted (2011), the facility had a busy program of events, filling six exhibition areas with a regularly changing calendar of travelling and in-house curated exhibitions[2] as well as developing appropriate public programs. The fully integrated staff structure offered a unique example of convergence for this research.

A detailed overview of the history, development and operational concerns of Westlands is available through successive function (i.e. business) plans for the institution produced between 2005 (before the opening of the new facility) and 2011, when the interviews for this research took place.

While it is not necessary to reiterate the contents of each plan (especially as each version contains significant repetition of previous documents), a brief analysis of the first function plan illustrates important issues that influenced the development and general operations of the institution at its inception and for the next five years, leading up to the point when the organisation became a case study for this research.

The executive summary of the first function plan, written in 2005, clearly articulated ambitious goals for the facility, namely the expectation that the opening would result in immediate benefits in cultural tourism and community pride, with a new facility providing a range of dynamic programs and services for both local residents and visitors to the area (Westlands function plan 2005, 1). As such, the imminent opening was hailed as a milestone for the wider geographical region. The objectives of the institution were to foster 'active engagement in cultural heritage and the arts' through an innovative, inspirational and welcoming facility that would preserve and exhibit its collections, as well as providing 'extensive learning opportunities' for the community (Ibid. Section 2.1).

From the outset, the function plan flagged the need for the newly built facility to justify its relevance to the district, stating that, through its vibrant programs, 'the museum and gallery will prove the importance of the centre to the local residential and tourist communities' (Ibid. Section 1). This somewhat peculiar choice of words seems to indicate that the new organisation was either not unanimously supported in the local community or the council's decision to proceed with its development had been met with scepticism from local residents.

The manager of the facility at that time (who authored the plan) signalled early doubts about the ability of the organisation to successfully deliver on expectations and remain sustainable in the longer term based on current staffing levels. In particular, she highlighted the increased size of the exhibition area, the large number of planned exhibitions and the lack of dedicated personnel to deliver educational programs, as well as unknown building maintenance costs, as areas of potential difficulty. At the time of opening, there were only five staff members employed, all working full-time.[3] The function plan identified the need to double that number. Likewise, a SWOT analysis provided in the plan identified the 'small professional team' and 'insufficient resources for research and development' among the centre's weaknesses, and identified a financial threat, noting the 'centre's requirements exceeds [*sic*] Council's operational budget' (Ibid. Section 4.1). The first function plan set out the important issues for the institution: ambitious programs and the anticipation of numerous benefits for the local community, the need for the facility to deliver positive outcomes to validate its existence and, simultaneously, emerging anxieties about the ongoing viability of these high expectations in view of the resources available to the institution.

Subsequent function plans continued to highlight the importance of these issues. On the one hand, the institution had committed staff and remained focussed on achieving its programming goals. On the other, the need to increase staff numbers was reiterated in the 2007/08 function plan, which also cited the need to secure private sponsorship, with the understanding that the city council would 'not cover the full cost of the centre indefinitely' (Westlands function plan 2007/08 executive summary). With perceptive insight, the author of this document highlighted the danger of a serious imbalance developing between the high standard and expectations set by the new building and the potential for the quality of programs to diminish, stating:

> Without support staff, services will be reduced and staff burn out will result . . . [The city] has an opportunity to be a leader in cultural programming given the capital investment in the building, but will rely on increased human resources to do so.
> (Ibid. executive summary)[4]

The final version of the 2007/08 plan reinforced the apprehension surrounding the sustainability of the institution's programs, also stating that the facility's resources requirement 'exceeds Council's operational budget beyond 2010,' even while the marketing strategy detailed in the same document locked the institution into a cycle of constantly changing exhibitions as a key selling point.[5] The 2009/10 function plan, which included budget details and a ten-year financial plan, listed an operational deficit of almost $2 million for the organisation – a total that was projected to grow steadily through to 2019.

By the end of 2009, the publication of the 2010/11 function plan appeared to show a stabilisation in the operations of the organisation. The outgoing manager wrote,

> Resources at both human and financial levels are sound, team morale is high, the facility is very well regarded within the community and

industry and [place name removed] city council is committed to ensuring its sustainability.

(Westlands function plan 2010/11 executive summary: 3)

One year later, the 2011/12 function plan, authored by the new manager, painted a slightly different picture of the institution. In his executive summary, he noted that visitation figures had increased, with venue hire and educational programs representing the strengths of the organisation. At the same time, he observed that the institution's 'aggressive' schedule of exhibitions and programs would be difficult to sustain at current staffing levels.

Lonehill Library, Museum and Gallery

Lonehill represents convergence on a considerably larger scale than that of Westlands. Also located in regional NSW, the city where Lonehill is located has an immediate population of around 50,000, with a median age of 37. The city is a hub for a network of rural centres.

Funded through the local council, Lonehill is a convergence of the city library, regional museum and regional art gallery. The library and museum, as well as a new technology and information section, share a building 'with limited barriers between the zones . . . to encourage integration of spaces and experiences' (conference paper delivered by Lonehill senior staff member 2009, 10). According to its collections policy (2011), the organisation aims to stimulate community engagement and interest in all forms of culture, and the heritage of the region, through innovative exhibitions, programs and publications.

The foundations for the formation of this institution were laid in the late 1990s, with strategic planning at council level suggesting the development of a cultural precinct in the city centre as well as the co-location of the existing library and museum[6] to achieve economies of scale across the two facilities. In addition, the thematic relationships across the library, museum and local studies collections and the joint purpose of collecting organisations in providing educational opportunities (as well as emerging technological capabilities to streamline collection access) provided further justification for the integration of cultural services. In the course of their research into the integration of cultural services, council staff became interested in adopting a fully converged model for the management and staffing of a new, joint institution (conference paper delivered by Lonehill senior staff member 2009, 11–12). New funding opportunities for convergence projects from state and federal governments provided the final impetus for the decision to amalgamate facilities and services.

Lonehill was opened in 2007 and, at the time of the research, employed the full-time equivalent of approximately 25 staff, including two management staff at council. Multiple exhibition and research areas existed within the main building, with the aim of encouraging audiences to engage in a variety of library, museum and research experiences. The management structure extended across to the regional gallery, located nearby. The goal of integrated collection access was addressed with the development of an online search engine that functioned across the library, museum and art gallery databases. Furthermore, the institution's education team was working across all facets of the organisation, devising public programs to take advantage of all the collections and spaces available.

Internal review documents from 2010 and 2011 reveal that the art gallery and museum were regularly hosting in excess of 30 exhibitions every year – around half of which were curated in-house – with five exhibition spaces at the gallery and another five at the combined library and museum venue. In 2011, the council's intention was to further increase the total number. The council's cultural plan for 2011–2013 stated that about 25,000 people visited the gallery, 45,000 attended museum exhibitions and almost 200,000 used the library facilities, indicating that the library component was the most popular aspect of the convergence (although it was not clear what percentage of these library figures represented multiple return visits).

A number of positive indicators attest to the success of the new institution in attracting local visitors and becoming a popular destination within the city centre. Attendance figures revealed that the combined museum and library facility was enjoying around double the visitation of the previous library and museum (conference paper delivered by Lonehill senior staff member 2009, 10). A user survey conducted in 2010 reported widespread satisfaction with the institution, citing 'the opportunity to offer an enhanced environment, more extensive exhibitions and public programs, improved public access technology and . . . a wider and more recent book stock' among the key advantages.[7] In addition, a large number of visitors used more than one service provided by the institution, although library and computer/internet usage were the most popular activities.

However, the function of the institution proved challenging from an operational perspective. In the four years since opening,[8] the organisational structure had already undergone four revisions, gradually breaking down from a fully converged staffing model to a more traditional, domain-based division of departments and role descriptions. In a conference paper delivered only two years after the opening of Lonehill, a manager working in the institution conceded that the converged structure was experimental and had already been subject to review. This staff member referred to the administration of the institution as 'making it up as we went along,' suggesting that the implementation of the converged institutional model was untried and constantly evolving. Furthermore, the same manager noted that the reorganisation of staff into new roles created with the convergence was not always successful, with numerous members of staff being unqualified or inexperienced for their new responsibilities – a situation compounded by inadequate change management and poorly defined role descriptions (conference paper 2008).

Owing to regular changes to the organisational structure, responsibility for the collections at Lonehill shifted between staff with expertise in diverse professional areas, with mixed results for collection care and interpretation. For example, in the initial converged structure, the collections manager role became responsible for holdings across the museum and gallery and the library's local studies collection. One consequence of the placement of staff in roles outside of their expertise was the underutilisation of the museum and gallery collections for exhibitions and a temporary stall in collection development (blog comments by senior staff member 2010). Similarly, the implementation of cross-collection management strategies prompted concerns about the dilution of professionalism and specialist expertise at the institution (Ibid.). In 2011, an audit of the visual arts collection found a significant cataloguing backlog, inconsistent documentation of the art collection and inadequate procedures for collection management (Lonehill cultural services strategic plan 2011–2013, 6). This audit did not, however, specify whether these shortcomings had occurred because of insufficient staffing, staff expertise or resources since the convergence, or whether the situation was inherited from the previously autonomous art gallery administration.

Through its wording, it appears that the 2011–2013 cultural services strategic plan moved to harmonise some of the tensions and discords within the organisation as a result of the convergence and ongoing restructuring. The document listed ideals such as mutual respect, teamwork, communication between teams, continued professional development and a commitment to 'positive incremental change' among the institution's core values.

Many of the existing staff members at Lonehill had worked in the institution since before it was opened and had experienced the various staffing restructures. In this way, they were able to provide direct insight into the impact of convergence on staff roles, the capacity of professionals to work outside of their area of expertise and the development of new skills for working in a converged institution.

Maunga Tapu Museum, Library and Visitor Centre

Opened in 2003, Maunga Tapu is a converged city library, regional museum and visitor information centre, also incorporating a research centre that uses museum, library and archival resources. The institution is located in the town centre of a regional district of New Zealand with a population of around 70,000 people. People of Maori descent comprise about 15% of the local population.

Both the public library and museum and co-location of these institutions had a relatively long history in the area. Both were established (as separate entities) in the early twentieth century.⁹ Around 1960, the two organisations moved into the same building. However, the inadequacy of the existing space for both the museum and the library's staff and activities was recognised within a decade (documented in a council review of Maunga Tapu 1998, 1–5). It was not until 1989, when the museum came under the auspices of the district council, that discussion about an improved facility could proceed in earnest.

According to the facility's website, the concept for the converged organisation first developed in 1993 when a council working party was formed to explore solutions for the lack of space and storage at the library and museum. At this time, only a small percentage of the museum collection could be displayed. Concluding a decade-long planning process, the council determined that a new building would be constructed and that the museum and library would move beyond co-location to become an integrated cultural heritage institution, providing seamless access to library, museum and archival collections. In 1995, the council decided to construct the new building on a site significant to both Maori and colonial settler histories. Council contribution to the project was NZ$12.7 million, with fit-out to be funded through non-council contributions. Around 2002, during the construction of the building, it was decided that a visitor information (tourism) service would also be added to the facility.

The development of the institution was not without its controversies. The proposed facility was not immediately supported by ratepayers, with many opposed to increases in council rates and unclear about the benefits of improved cultural services. A community consultation process was undertaken by the council and produced 'vigorous debate,' resulting in hundreds of written and verbal submissions (council review of Maunga Tapu 1998). The predominant concern among those who expressed negative opinions appeared to centre on the substantial project costs. Through an information campaign, the district council justified the capital cost of the project by anticipating that facilities and staff could be shared across the library and museum facilities (Ibid. 23), as well as taking advantage of economies of scale. By implementing this integrated strategy, it was thought that the overall space requirement of the new building would be reduced, as well as minimising the number of necessary employees.

Proponents of the development argued the need for an up-to-date, larger building, citing the responsibility of the museum to make its locally significant collections as accessible as possible to the community. Furthermore, an enhanced capacity to articulate historical and cultural narratives through exhibitions became central to the planning of the new museum: 'There is a need to ensure that the story of [place name removed], its environment, people and events is told as a service both to residents and visitors' (council review of Maunga Tapu 1998, 8). These aims were to be achieved by doubling the existing space, where the museum and library would collaborate to create one 'knowledge centre' offering a variety of services (wording used in a conference paper delivered by a former manager of Maunga Tapu 2008).

The emphasis of the convergence between the library and the museum was on educational offerings, information retrieval, collection storage, research and improved access. The idea was to provide 'combined access to collections, combined programming and a research facility' (Maunga Tapu conference proceedings 2006, 14) where public library, museum and visitor information services would 'flow from one to another through the sharing of knowledge' (Maunga Tapu visitor brochure c.2011). According to fundraising documents (c.1998), the plan for the institution was to harness new technologies to create networked databases across various information resources, as well as using technology for interactive displays. Key nodes for the delivery of integrated services were the research centre (focussing on local history resources), children's discovery area and the institution's website.

Convergence at Maunga Tapu was perceived as a solution to achieving the most cost-effective realisation of the project, as well as delivering cultural benefits in enabling improved access to collections and information resources, leading to increased knowledge of the history and identity of the region. Funding proceeded, with the council's outlay of NZ$12.7 million for the build supplemented by funds for the fit-out and ongoing exhibition expenses from national government sectors, adding NZ$4.2 million. Corporate and other forms of private sponsorships yielded a further approximately NZ$11.5 million. The total project cost was about NZ$26.5 million.

The fundraising documents produced to garner the support of the local community, as well as attract sponsorship from corporate partners, reveal the ambitious goals of the project, citing far-reaching advantages for both users of the institution and the wider community. One brochure produced for the sponsorship campaign (c.1998) highlighted the integration of museum and library visitor experiences across the facility, envisaging that visitors would adopt a holistic approach to utilising all the resources that the institution had to offer. It stated, 'Visitors will be able to move from exhibits and halls into research rooms – take a close-up look at artefacts, then explore interactive media throughout the facility or retrieve detailed information from the library.' Another information pamphlet (c.2000) targeting the general public stressed the need for a cultural centre that could effectively communicate the significant narratives of the region through extensive displays and innovative access points to information. The institution was heralded as the 'world's first integrated museum, library and tourist information centre' (Maunga Tapu website 'History' section 2008), offering a best practice approach to the presentation of cultural heritage (Maunga Tapu information brochure c.1998, 1; Maunga Tapu fundraising document 2008, 10). It was promoted as 'an innovative model of knowledge centre,' where services would be converged to foster 'knowledge provision' (Maunga Tapu conference proceedings 2006, 1). Furthermore, it would boost the regeneration of the town centre and assist in creating a 'heart' of the city (Ibid.: 7). Finally, the institution would be instrumental in driving creativity and innovation in the community and would stimulate the 'knowledge economy' and promote 'social well-being,' 'environmental well-being' and 'economic well-being' (conference paper delivered by a former manager, Maunga Tapu 2008).

The 2003 high-profile opening of the architecturally prominent institution seemed to have achieved many of these aims. The new building boasted approximately 10,000 square metres of space, with substantial exhibition areas allocated to both permanent and temporary displays, including a significant allotment for the exhibition of a large collection of Maori artefacts. However, it is unclear to what extent the institution genuinely lived up to its ideals, with both the space and the organisational structure only partly embodying the idea of convergence.

The library and museum remained as effectively separate buildings, with a research centre and gallery creating both a physical and conceptual link between the two functions. In terms of organisational structure (Maunga Tapu management report 2008), the overall manager role for the institution oversaw both the library and the museum, with the next tier of administration spread across four roles covering library, museum, business development and exhibitions, respectively. The library service was allocated almost 50% of the staffing resources, while the heritage collections (museum) accounted for only 9% and exhibitions approximately 4%. On the surface, these statistics suggest that the library was effectively operating as the dominant partner within the institution's structure.

After the first five years of its operation, Maunga Tapu's management and the local council realised the inadequacy of the initial revenue to cover costs into the future, launching another round of fundraising for ongoing operational, collection management and exhibition development costs. The booklet published for this campaign notes the achievements of the institution but also highlights the need for greater investment in expert curatorial staff to address a substantial cataloguing backlog. Written in 2008, it acknowledged that the full narrative potential of the heritage collections had yet to be realised, implicitly admitting that the aim of the institution to 'tell the stories of the region' had not yet been achieved. The booklet stated,

> For every heritage item we have in public catalogues ten are waiting. They are safe and secure, but incredibly, nobody fully knows what we hold in our collections. . . . It will only come to light as expert curatorial resources become available.

It is not clear, however, whether this situation developed through inadequate forward planning, an inappropriate organisational structure or an imbalance in resources allocated to various sections of the institution.

Notes

1 Accurate at July 2011, when interviews were conducted.
2 The organisation's 2009 collection policy outlined the expected exhibition schedule across the institution, with the main visual arts gallery turning over every 6 to 8 weeks and the temporary museum space hosting new exhibitions every 12 to 16 weeks, with displays in the smaller exhibition areas also subject to change.
3 By 2009, the staff number had increased to approximately 7.5 full-time equivalent, including non–collection-based roles such as administration and site maintenance. At this time, the institution was also responsible for coordinating 115 volunteer 'ambassadors' and venue hire for the community arts centre facility. The 2009/10 function plan still listed insufficient staffing and long-term sustainability as important issues for the organisation.
4 For greater detail, see also Section 4: 19–20.
5 The institution's collection policy, included in the 2007/08 function plan, further highlights that the 'fundamental role of [Westlands] is to provide access to quality exhibition and cultural material.'
6 In various forms and locations, a local museum had existed in the city since the late nineteenth century. In the early 1980s, the council assumed responsibility for the museum collections from the district historical society.
7 This survey did not include art gallery patrons.
8 At May 2011, when interviews were conducted.
9 Both a public library and the museum collection came into being in the mid-nineteenth century. The museum collection grew through the early twentieth century with the addition of some substantial private collections, including one containing a large number of significant Maori artefacts. Meanwhile, the library also developed with the provision of new facilities in 1908 and 1918.

Appendix 2
Case study comparative table

Case Study Title	Location	Year est.	Initial capital cost	Type of convergence	Annual operating budget (approx.)	Staff (full-time equiv.)	Staff interviewed	Interviewee job titles
WESTLANDS Museum, Gallery & Arts Centre	Regional NSW	2006	$8.2M	Regional museum, regional art gallery, community arts centre	Unknown	7–8	8	Manager; Centre Coordinator; Collections Officer; Curator; Assistant Curator; Education Officer; Community Services Director, City Council; Local Studies Officer
LONEHILL Library, Museum & Gallery	Regional NSW	2007	$15.2M (library and museum building only)	City library, regional museum, regional art gallery	AUS $5.3M (incl. branch library & entertainment centre)	25	12	Visual Arts Coordinator; Museum and Social History Coordinator; Collections and Exhibitions Officer; Library Manager; Cultural Services, Customer Service & Operations Coordinator; Learning and Outreach Coordinator; Group Leader, Cultural Services, City Council; Exhibitions Coordinator; Information and Library Collections Coordinator; Cultural Development Officer, City Council; Team Leader, Art Gallery and Collections; Learning and Outreach Officer

(*Continued*)

(Continued)

Case Study Title	Location	Year est.	Initial capital cost	Type of convergence	Annual operating budget (approx.)	Staff (full-time equiv.)	Staff interviewed	Interviewee job titles
MAUNGA TAPU Museum, Library & Visitor Centre	NZ	2003	NZ $26.5M	Regional museum, regional library, visitor information centre	NZ $10M	78	10	CEO, District Council; Former Manager; Acting Manager; Exhibitions Project and Technical Administrator; Exhibitions Manager; Research Manager; Manager of Heritage Collections; Curator of Pictorial Collections; Pictorial Collections Technician; Curator of Archives

Bibliography

Annis, S. 1994. "The Museum as a Staging Ground for Symbolic Action." In *Museum Provision and Professionalism*, edited by G. Kavanagh, 21–25. London: Routledge.
Bal, M. 2004. "Telling Objects: A Narrative Perspective on Collecting." In *Grasping the World: The Idea of the Museum*, edited by D. Preziosi and C. Farago. Aldershot: Ashgate Publishing Ltd.
Bastian, J.A. and R. Harvey. 2012. "The Convergence of Cultural Heritage: Practical Experiments and Lessons Learned." In *The Memory of the World in the Digital Age: Digitization and Preservation – An International Conference on Permanent Access to Digital Documentary Heritage*. Vancouver: UNESCO.
Batchelor, R. 1994. "Not Looking at Kettles." In *Interpreting Objects and Collections*, edited by S. Pearce, 139–43. London: Routledge.
Baum, N. 2008. Submission No.76 (Local Government Association of NSW and the Shires Association of NSW), *Inquiry into Development of Arts and Cultural Infrastructure Outside the Sydney CBD*. Sydney: NSW Parliament, Legislative Assembly, Standing Committee on Public Works.
Beasley, G. 2007. "Curatorial Crossover: Building Library, Archives, and Museum Collections." *RBM: A Journal of Rare Books, Manuscripts, and Cultural Heritage* 8: 20–8.
Bennett, T. 1995. *The Birth of the Museum: History, Theory, Politics*. London and New York: Routledge.
Bettington, J., Eberhard, K., Loo, R. and C. Smith, eds. 2008. *Keeping Archives*. Canberra: Australian Society of Archivists.
Bickersteth, J. 2010. "Collaboration and Convergence 15 June 2010." *Museum Musings*. Accessed July 5, 2010. http://bickersteth.blogspot.com/2010/06/collaboration-and-convergence.html
Boaden, S. and C. Clement. 2009. "Beyond Co-location to Convergence: Designing and Managing New Model Public Library Spaces and Services to Reflect Trends in Convergence and Integration." *IFLA Preconference Satellite: Libraries as Space and Place*. Turin: IFLA.
Boylan, P.J. 2006. "Current Trends in Governance and Management of Museums in Europe." In *Museum Philosophy for the Twenty-First Century*, edited by H.H. Genoways. Oxford: AltaMira Press.

Buckland, M.K. 1991. "Information as Thing." *Journal of the American Society for Information Science* 42: 351–60.
Byrne, D. 2013. "Love & Loss in the 1960s." *International Journal of Heritage Studies* 19 (6): 596–609.
Byrum, J.D. 1997. "Introduction." In *ISBD(ER): International Standard Bibliographic Description for Electronic Resources*, edited by J.D. Byrum, S. Hedberg, C. Marandas, M.L Martinez-Conde, and A.M. Sandberg-Fox. Munich: K.G. Saur.
Carr, D. 2006. "Mind as Verb." In *Museum philosophy for the Twenty-First Century*, edited by H. Genoways. Oxford: AltaMira Press.
Chinn, C. 2010. "Shifts in Power and Authority." *UpNext: The Future of Museums and Libraries* [Online]. Accessed April 27, 2010. http://imlsupnext.wikispaces.com/Theme+2-+Shifts+in+Power+%26+Authority
Chung, J., S. Wilkening, and S. Johnstone. 2008. *Museums & Society 2034: Trends and Potential Futures*. Center for the Future of Museums. Washington, DC: American Association of Museums.
CILIP. 2009. *Beyond the Silos of the LAMs: Unlocking the Benefits of Collaboration Between Libraries, Archives and Museums*. London. Accessed September 9, 2009. www.cilip.org.uk/interests/execbriefings/lams/index.html
Clareson, T. 2016. *Mapping the Landscapes Focus Group Final Report*. Washington, DC: Institute of Museum and Library Services (IMLS)/Coalition to Advance Learning in Archives, Libraries, and Museums.
Clement, C. 2007. "Cultural Heart." In *The MAG*. Sydney: Museums and Galleries NSW.
Coburn, E. et al. 2010. "The Cataloguing Cultural Objects experience: Codifying Practice for the Cultural Heritage Community." *IFLA Journal* 36: 16–29.
Cook, T. 2009. "The Archive(s) Is a Foreign Country: Historians, Archivists, and the Changing Archival Landscape." *The Canadian Historical Review* 90: 497–534.
Crane, S.A. 2011. "The Conundrum of Ephemerality: Time, Memory, and Museums." In *A Companion to Museum Studies*, edited by S. Macdonald. Oxford: Blackwell Publishing.
Crossick, G. and P. Kaszynska. 2016. *Understanding the Value of Arts and Culture: The AHRC Cultural Value Project*. Swindon: Arts and Humanities Research Council.
Curry, D.R. 2010a. *One Potential Future for Museums, Archives, Libraries*. Accessed April 13, 2010. http://futureofmuseums.blogspot.com/2010/03/one-potential-future-for-museums.html
Curry, D.R. 2010b. *Thinking About Convergence Part 2: The Knowledge Commons*. Center for the Future of Museums. Accessed August 2, 2010. http://futureofmuseums.blogspot.com/2010/03/thinking-about-convergence-part-2.html
Davis, P. 2007. "Ecomuseums and Sustainability in Italy, Japan and China." In *Museum Revolutions: How Museums Change and Are Changed*, edited by S. Knell, S. Macleod, and S. Watson. London: Routledge.
Davis, W. and K. Howard. 2013. "Cultural Policy and Australia's National Cultural Heritage: Issues and Challenges in the GLAM Landscape." *The Australian Library Journal* 62 (1): 15–26.

De Laurentis, C. 2006. "Digital Knowledge Exploitation: ICT, Memory Institutions and Innovation from Cultural Assets." *Journal of Technology Transfer* 31: 77–79.

Dempsey, L. 2000. "Scientific, Industrial, and Cultural Heritage: A Shared Approach: A Research Framework for Digital Libraries, Museums and Archives." *Ariadne* 22. Accessed August 2, 2012. www.ariadne.ac.uk/issue22/dempsey/

Don, N. 2008. Submission No.21 (Public Libraries NSW - Country), *Inquiry into Development of Arts and Cultural Infrastructure Outside the Sydney CBD*. Sydney: NSW Parliament, Legislative Assembly, Standing Committee on Public Works.

Doucet, M. 2007. "Library and Archives Canada: A Case Study of a National Library, Archives and Museum Merger." *RBM: A Journal of Rare Books, Manuscripts and Cultural Heritage* 8: 61–66.

Drummond, C. et al., eds. 2016. *National Agenda for Continuing Education and Professional Development Across Libraries, Archives and Museums*. Dublin, OH: OCLC Research. www.oclc.org/content/dam/research/publications/2016/oclcresearch-national-agenda- lams-education-development-2016.pdf

Dudley, S.H., ed. 2010. *Museum Materialities: Objects, Engagements, Interpretations*. New York: Routledge.

Duff, W.M., J. Carter, J.M. Cherry, H. MacNeil, and L.C. Howarth. 2013. "From Coexistence to Convergence: Studying Partnerships and Collaboration Among Libraries, Archives and Museums." *Information Research* 18, paper 585.

Dunphy, K. 2010. "How Can the Impact of Cultural Development Work in Local Government Be Measured? Towards More Effective Planning and Evaluation Strategies." *Local Global* 7: 100–18.

Elliot, R. et al. 1994. "Towards a Material History Methodology." In *Interpreting Objects and Collections*, edited by S. Pearce, 109–24. London: Routledge.

Enser, P. 2001. "On Continuity, Culture, Competition – Cooperation and Convergence, Too." *New Library World* 102: 423–29.

Featherstone, M., 2006. "Archive." *Theory, Culture & Society* 23 (2–3): 591–96.

Findlen, P. 2004. "The Museum: Its Classical Etymology and Renaissance Genealogy." In *Grasping the World: The Idea of the Museum*, edited by D. Preziosi and C. Farago. Aldershot: Ashgate Publishing Ltd.

Freeman, O. and R. Watson, 2009. *The Bookends Scenarios: Alternative Futures for the Public Library Network in NSW in 2030*. Sydney: State Library of NSW.

Genoways, H.H. 2006. "To Members of the Museum Profession." In *Museum Philosophy for the Twenty-First Century*, edited by H.H. Genoways. Oxford: AltaMira Press.

Gibson, H., A. Morris, and M. Cleeve. 2007. "Links Between Libraries and Museums: Investigating Museum-Library Collaboration in England and the USA." *Libri* 57: 53–64.

Given, L.M. and L. McTavish. 2010. "What's Old Is New Again: The Reconvergence of Libraries, Archives, and Museums in the Digital Age." *The Library Quarterly* 80: 7–32.

Glow, H. and K. Johanson. 2006. "Looking for Cultural Value: Critiques of Australian Cultural Policy." *Asia Pacific Journal of Arts and Cultural Management* 4 (2): 259–69.

Bibliography

Golanska, D. 2015. "Affective Spaces, Sensuous Engagements: In Quest of a Synaesthetic Approach to 'Dark Memorials'." *International Journal of Heritage Studies* 21 (8): 773–90.

Golding, V. and W. Modest, eds. 2013. *Museums and Communities: Curators, Collections, Collaboration*. London: Bloomsbury.

Gomez, M. 2010. "Changing Definitions and Roles of Museums and Libraries." *UpNext: The Future of Museums and Libraries* [Online]. Accessed April 27, 2010. http://imlsupnext.wikispaces.com/Theme+1-+Changing+Definitions+and+Roles+of+Museums+and+Libraries

Gordon, R.B. 1993. "The Interpretation of Artifacts in the History of Technology." In *History from Things: Essays on Material Culture*, edited by S. Lubar and D. Kingery, 74–93. Washington, DC: Smithsonian Institution Press.

Gray, C., 2002. "Local Government and the Arts." *Local Government Studies* 28 (1): 77–90.

Gray, C. 2017. "Local Government and the Arts revisited." *Local Government Studies* 43 (3): 315–22.

Griffiths, J.M. and D.W. King. 2008. *InterConnections: The IMLS National Study of the Use of Libraries, Museums and the Internet – Conclusions*. Institute of Museum and Library Services.

Halpin, M.M. 1997. " 'Play It Again, Sam': Reflections on a New Museology." *Museum International* 49 (2): 52–56.

Hedstrom, M. and J.L. King. 2004. "On the LAM: Library, Archive, and Museum Collections in the Creation and Maintenance of Knowledge Communities." In *Mapping Innovation: Six Depth Studies*. Organization for Economic Co-operation and Development.

Heumann G., E. 2010. "Curator: From Soloist to Impresario." In *Hot Topics, Public Culture, Museums*, edited by Fiona Cameron and Lynda Kelly, 95–111. Newcastle: Cambridge Scholars.

Hildreth, S. 2010. "Museums and Libraries as the Third Place." *UpNext: The Future of Museums and Libraries* [Online]. Accessed April 27, 2010. http://imlsupnext.wikispaces.com/Theme+3-+Museums+and+Libraries+as+the+Third+Place

Hislop, D. 2002. "Mission Impossible? Communicating and Sharing Knowledge via Information Technology." *Journal of Information Technology* 17: 165–77.

Hjorland, B. 2000. "Documents, Memory Institutions and Information Science." *Journal of Documentation* 56: 27–41.

Hooper-Greenhill, E. 1992. *Museums and the Shaping of Knowledge*. London: Routledge.

Hooper-Greenhill, E. 2000. "Objects and Interpretative Processes." In *Museums and the Interpretation of Visual Culture*, edited by E. Hooper-Greenhill. New York: Routledge.

Hutchison, M. 2013. "Shared Authority: Collaboration, Curatorial Voice, and Exhibition Design in Canberra, Australia." In *Museums and Communities: Curators, Collections, Collaboration*, edited by V. Golding and W. Modest, 143–62. London: Bloomsbury.

International Council of Museums (ICOM). 2007. "Museum Definition." In *ICOM International Council of Museums: The World Museum Community*

(website). Accessed November 17, 2017. http://icom.museum/the-vision/museum-definition/
Johnston, P. and B. Robinson. 2001. "Collection Convergence: The Work of the Collection Description Focus." *Ariadne* 29.
Jones, W. 2010. "No Knowledge but Through Information." *First Monday*, 15.
Jung, Y. 2016. "Micro Examination of Museum Workplace Culture: How Institutional Changes Influence the Culture of a Real-World Art Museum." *Museum Management and Curatorship* 31 (2): 159–77.
Kirchhoff, T., W. Schweibenz, and J. Sieglerschmidt. 2008. Archives, Libraries, Museums and the Spell of Ubiquitous Knowledge. *Archival Science* 8: 251–66.
Kreps, C.F. 2008. "Appropriate Museology in Theory and Practice." *Museum Management and Curatorship* 23 (1): 23–41.
Lipsky, M. 1980. *Street-level Bureaucracy: Dilemmas of the Individual in Public Services*. New York: Russell Sage Foundation.
Local Government NSW (LGNSW). 2017. *Communities and Culture: LGNSW Research into Arts, Culture and Heritage*. Sydney: NSW Government, LGNSW.
Lubar, S.D. and W.D. Kingery, eds. 1993. *History from Things: Essays on Material Culture*. Washington, DC: Smithsonian Institution Press.
Lynch, B.T. and Samuel J.M.M. Alberti. 2010. "Legacies of Prejudice: Racism, Co-Production and Radical Trust in the Museum." *Museum Management and Curatorship* 25 (1): 13–35.
Macdonald, S. 2006. "Expanding Museum Studies: An Introduction." In *A Companion to Museum Studies*, edited by S. Macdonald. Oxford: Blackwell Publishing.
Maciel, M.E. 2006. "The Unclassifiable." *Theory, Culture & Society* 23: 47–50.
Macnaught, B. 2008. *Podcast of Seminar Given at Powerful Places Conference*. Tamworth: Museums & Galleries NSW. Accessed March 3, 2009. http://mgnsw.org.au/data/podcasts/277/2_Bill_Macnaught.mp3
Madsen, C. 2010. *Library, Archive, and Museum Convergence*. Accessed April 13, 2010. http://christinemadsen.com/2010/library-archive-and-museum-convergence/
Marsden, C. 2001. "Sectors and Domains: Some Reflections on Co-operation and Integration." *Journal of the Society of Archivists* 22: 17–23.
Martin, R.S. 2007. "Intersecting Missions, Converging Practice." *RBM: A Journal of Rare Books, Manuscripts and Cultural Heritage* 8: 80–88.
Marty, P.F. 2008. *Cultural Heritage Information Professionals (CHIPS) Workshop Report*. Sarasota: Institute of Museum and Library Services (IMLS) Florida State University.
Matassa, F. 2011. *Museum Collections Management: A Handbook*. London: Facet Publishing.
Mayrand, P. 2015. "The New Museology Proclaimed." *Museum International* (261–264): 115–18.
McCall, V. and C. Gray. 2014. "Museums and the 'New Museology': Theory, Practice and Organisational Change." *Museum Management and Curatorship* 29 (1): 19–35.
McCarthy, C. 2015. "Introduction." In *Museum Practice*, edited by Conal McCarthy; Macdonald, Sharon, Helen Rees Leahy, Andrea Witcomb, Kylie Message, Conal

McCarthy, Michelle Henning, Annie E. Coombes, and Ruth B. Phillips. 2015. *The International Handbooks of Museum Studies*. 1st ed. Chichester, West Sussex: John Wiley & Sons Ltd.

McClung Fleming, E. 1982. "Artifact Study: A Proposed Model." In *Material Culture Studies in America*, edited by T.J. Schlereth. Nashville: American Association for State and Local History.

McKitterick, D. 2006. "Libraries and the Organisation of Knowledge." In *The Cambridge History of Libraries in Britain and Ireland*, edited by E. Leedham-Green and T. Webber. Cambridge: Cambridge University Press.

Miller, P. 2000. *A Little Bit of Joined-up Thinking: Some Issues of Convergence in Our Memory Institutions*. Paris: European Libraries Automation Group.

Mulcahy, K. 2006. "Cultural Policy: Definitions and Theoretical Approaches." *Journal of Arts Management, Law and Society* 35 (4): 319–30.

Mulligan, M. and P. Smith. 2010. "Art, Governance and the Turn to Community: Key Findings of the Research on the Generations Project." *Local Global* 7: 34–40.

Murphy, S.A. 2005. "The Reference Narrative." *Reference & User Services Quarterly* 44: 247–52.

Neal, J.G. 2007. "Global Collaboration and the Future of the OCLC Cooperative." *Libraries and the Academy* 7: 263–71.

Olson, H.A. 2001. "The Power to Name: Representation in Library Catalogues." *Signs* 26: 639–68.

Onciul, Bryony. 2013. "Community Engagement, Curatorial Practice, and Museum Ethos in Alberta, Canada." In *Museums and Communities: Curators, Collections, Collaboration*, edited by Vivien Golding and Wayne Modest, 79–97. London: Bloomsbury.

Panofsky, E. 1970. *Iconography and Iconology: An Introduction to the Study of Renaissance Art. Meaning in the Visual Arts*. Harmondsworth: Penguin Books.

Paquet K., R. 2016. "Inclusion in Museums: A Matter of Social Justice." *Museum Management and Curatorship*. Advance online publication. doi:10.1080/09647775.2016.1211960.

Paris, S.G. 2006. "How Can Museums Attract Visitors in the Twenty-First Century?" In *Museum Philosophy for the Twenty-First Century*, edited by H.H. Genoways. Oxford: AltaMira Press.

Patchen, J. H. 2006. "Defining Our Museum Audience: An Extraordinary Opportunity." In *Museum Philosophy for the Twenty-First Century*, edited by H.H. Genoways, 247–54. Oxford: AltaMira Press.

Peacock, D., D. Ellis, and J. Doolan. 2004. "Searching for Meaning: Not Just Records." In *Museums and the Web 2004*. Toronto, Canada.

Pearce, S., ed. 1994. *Interpreting Objects and Collections*. London: Routledge.

Pearce, S. 1999. "Collections and Collecting." In *Museums and the Future of Collecting*, edited by S.J. Knell. Aldershot: Ashgate Publishing Ltd.

Prown, J.D. 1994. "Mind in Matter: An Introduction to Material Culture Theory and Method." In *Interpreting Objects and Collections*, edited by S. Pearce. London: Routledge.

Robinson, H. 2018. Cultural Policy, Local Government and Museums: An Australian Perspective. *Local Government Studies*. doi:10.1080/03003930.2018.1488688.

Robison, A. 2007. "Curatorial Reflections on Print Rooms and Libraries." *RBM: A Journal of Rare Books, Manuscripts, and Cultural Heritage* 8 (1): 35–44.

Rozan, A. 2017. "Museums at 2040." *Museum 2040* (November/December): 16–21.

Ruis-Ulldemolins, J. 2016. "The Rise of the Hybrid Model of Art Museums and Cultural Institutions: The Case of Barcelona." *Museum Management and Curatorship* 31 (2): 178–92.

Russell, R. and K. Winkworth. 2009. *Significance 2.0: A Guide to Assessing the Significance of Collections.* Adelaide: Collections Council of Australia Ltd.

Sandell, R. 2011. "On Ethics, Activism and Human Rights." In *The Routledge Companion to Museum Ethics: Redefining Ethics for the Twenty-First-Century Museum*, edited by Janet Marstine. London and New York: Routledge.

Saurombe, N. and P. Ngulube. 2016. "To Collaborate or Not to Collaborate, That Is the Question: Raising the Profile of Public Archives in East and Southern Africa." *Information Development*, 1–20. doi:10.1177/0266666916684181.

Savage-Yamakazi, B. and N. Murrell. 2015. *Engage: The Future of Museums – Interim Findings from Roundtable Discussions on Audience Engagement and the Role of the Museum in the Community.* Chicago: Gensler Research. Accessed March 25, 2016. www.gensler.com/uploads/document/395/file/gensler_museum-research-interim-report.pdf

Schlereth, T., ed. 1982. *Material Culture Studies in America.* Nashville: American Association for State and Local History.

Scott, C. 2015. "Museum Measurement: Questions of Value." In *Museum Practice*, edited by C. McCarthy. Chichester, West Sussex: John Wiley & Sons Ltd.

Shelton, A. 2013. "Critical Museology: A Manifesto." *Museum Worlds: Advances in Research* 1: 7–23.

Simon, N. 2010. *The Participatory Museum.* Santa Cruz, CA: Museum 2.0.

Sola, T., 1997. *Essays on Museums and Their Theory: Towards a Cybernetic Museum.* Helsinki: Finnish Museums Association.

Stam, D.C. 1993. "The Informed Muse: The Implications of 'The New Museology' for Museum Practice." *Museum Management and Curatorship* 12: 267–83.

Stapleton, M. 2007. "Premium Blend." In *The MAG.* Sydney: Museums and Galleries NSW.

Stehr, N. and U. Ufer. 2009. "On the Global Distribution and Dissemination of Knowledge." *International Social Science Journal* 60: 7–24.

Tanackovic, S.F. and B. Badurina. 2009. "Collaboration of Croatian Cultural Heritage Institutions: Experiences for Museums." *Museum Management and Curatorship* 24: 299–321.

Taylor, A. 2016. "Powerhouse Inquiry Told Regional NSW a 'Cultural Ghetto of Poverty'." *Sydney Morning Herald*, September 26, 2016. Accessed September 18, 2017. www.smh.com.au/entertainment/art-and-design/powerhouse-inquiry-told-regional-nsw-a-cultural-ghetto-of-poverty-20160922-grlzla.html

Taylor, I. and J. Kelly. 2006. "Professionals, Discretion and Public Sector Reform in the UK: Re-visiting Lipsky." *International Journal of Public Sector Management* 19 (7): 629–42.

Trant, J. 2009. "Emerging Convergence? Thoughts on Museums, Archives, Libraries, and Professional Training." *Museum Management and Curatorship* 24: 369–87.

van Barnefeld, K. and O. Chiu. 2017. "A Portrait of Failure: Ongoing Funding Cuts to Australia's Cultural Institutions." *Australian Journal of Public Administration.* doi:10.1111/1467-8500.12248.

Venn, C. 2006. "The Collection." *Theory, Culture & Society* 23: 35–40.

Waibel, G. and Erway, R. 2009. "Think Globally, Act Locally: Library, Archive, and Museum Collaboration." *Museum Management and Curatorship* 24: 323–35.

Weil, S. 1999. "From Being About Something to Being for Somebody: The Ongoing Transformation of the American Museum." *Daedalus* 128: 229–58.

Wright, M. 2010. "New Models and Structures for Collaboration." *UpNext: The Future of Museums and Libraries* [Online]. Accessed April 27, 2010. http://imlsupnext.wikispaces.com/Theme+6-+New+Models+%26+Structures+for+Collaboration

Yakel, E., 2003. "Archival Representation." *Archival Science* 3 (1): 1–25.

Yakel, E., 2005. "Choices and Challenges: Cross-cutting Themes in Archives and Museums." *Archives and Manuscripts* 21 (1): 13–17.

Yakel, E. 2007. "Digital Curation." *Archives and Manuscripts* 23: 335–40.

Yarrow, A., B. Clubb, and J.L. Draper. 2008. "Public Libraries, Archives and Museums: Trends in Collaboration and Cooperation." In *International Federation of Library Associations and Institutions IFLA Professional Reports.* The Hague: IFLA.

Zorich, D., G. Waibel, and R. Erway. 2008. *Beyond the Silos of the LAMs: Collaboration Among Libraries, Archives and Museums.* Dublin, OH: OCLC Programs and Research.

Index

accessioning 34, 45, 50, 51, 63, 68, 107
acquisition of museum objects 6, 32, 35, 44, 45, 47, 48, 49, 66, 67, 89, 105
American Alliance of Museums 1
Annis, Sheldon 33
Arts and Humanities Research Council (AHRC) UK 9

Buckland, Michael 29–31

cataloguing 6, 13, 24, 27–8, 34, 36, 40, 49, 50–3, 55, 63–4, 66–7, 87, 98, 104, 106, 120, 123, 124
CILIP (Chartered Institute of Library and Information Professionals) 20–1
classification 13–14, 33–4, 36, 45, 105
co-location of facilities 11, 38, 106, 118, 121
Cook, Terry 35
cultural policy 2–5, 7–8, 19–20, 24, 38, 97, 106
cultural utilitarianism 2, 19
cultural value 2, 9, 107
curatorial authority 19

democratisation 18, 97
Dempsey, Lorcan 15, 26–7, 31, 110
Dewey Decimal Classification (DDC) 36
digital convergence 3, 11, 15–16, 25–7, 31, 38, 42, 52, 54, 110

Ecomuseums 20
economies of scale 3, 18, 74–5, 118, 121

efficiency 2, 16–19, 22, 42, 48, 50, 61, 65, 72, 75, 84, 93, 99, 102, 103, 108, 110
encyclopaedism 13
epistemology 13–15, 24–5, 28–9, 34–7, 53–4, 70
Europeana 3

Hislop, Donald 30–1, 106
Hooper-Greenhill, Eileen 12, 33, 35

Institute for Museums and Library Services (IMLS) USA 2, 12, 16, 20, 23
International Council of Museums (ICOM) 20
interpretive sustainability 4, 7, 25, 36, 38, 42, 68, 96–7, 106, 108, 111–13

Jones, William 30, 39, 106

knowledge institutions 6, 24, 31–6, 37, 41, 67, 98, 106

leadership 7, 71, 77–81
Library and Archives Canada 25
Library of Congress Subject Headings (LCSH) 36
Lipsky, Michael 44
local studies 46–7, 67–8, 72, 80

McCarthy, Conal 70, 108
metadata 11, 16
municipalisation of culture 17
Museums, Libraries and Archives Council (MLA) UK 2, 27

new museology 18–22, 111

Olson, Hope 36

Pearce, Susan 14, 32–3, 35
positivism 27, 31–2, 54
process conflict 6, 41, 67, 102, 109
productivity 2–3, 90, 102–4, 108
professional development 87, 92–3, 102, 109–10, 120

third place 20, 22, 116
Trove 3

urban renewal 2–3, 18

vocabularies 16, 28, 36

Weil, Stephen 19–20, 111–12

Yakel, Elizabeth 15, 35

For Product Safety Concerns and Information please contact our EU representative GPSR@taylorandfrancis.com
Taylor & Francis Verlag GmbH, Kaufingerstraße 24, 80331 München, Germany

www.ingramcontent.com/pod-product-compliance
Lightning Source LLC
Chambersburg PA
CBHW070738230426
43669CB00014B/2497